YOU CAN'T
PLAY THE GAME
IF YOU DON'T
KNOW
THE RULES

To my brother Keith, who, as an engineer, believes you should be able to explain how things work —especially with diagrams. And to my sons, Luke and Zac.

YOU CAN'T PLAY THE GAME IF YOU DON'T KNOW THE RULES

How Relationships Work

Irene Alexander

LION

A Lion Book
an imprint of
Lion Hudson plc
Wilkinson House, Jordan Hill Road,
Oxford OX2 8DR, England

www.lionhudson.com
ISBN 978 0 7459 5331 1 (UK)
ISBN 978 0 8254 7844 4 (US)
Distributed by:
UK: Marston Book Services, PO Box 269, Abingdon, Oxon, OX14 4YN
USA: Trafalgar Square Publishing, 814 N. Franklin Street, Chicago, IL 60610
USA: Christian Market: Kregel Publications, PO Box 2607, Grand Rapids,
Michigan 49501

First edition 2009
10 9 8 7 6 5 4 3 2 1 0

Acknowledgments
This book is almost entirely the work of other people, with a few additions of my own.
My contribution has been to summarise and collate, attempting to relate the ideas
to everyday life in everyday language. I have sought to acknowledge all sources and
accurately represent the original authors. To them I am grateful – not only for their work
which I quote, but for their influence in my own life.
I would also like to thank the numbers of people who have read and responded to this
manuscript. Michael Langton and Andrew Steel gave me some male perspectives.
My sister Elaine read every word and encouraged my writing – as did my mother.
My brother Keith inspired the book in the first place and critiqued my diagrams over
many lunches.
I am grateful too, to the staff of the University of Canterbury School of Engineering
and the Riccarton House coffee shop for their generous hospitality, giving me space
and beauty to write in.
And to Pieter and Sue from Piquant for their encouragement and networking –
Thank you!

A catalogue record for this book is available from the British Library
Typeset in 11/13 Bembo

Contents

Introduction:
Playing Football Blindfolded

Have you ever tried to explain the rules of a football or rugby match to someone from another culture? Or even an ordinary garden-variety woman like me who doesn't understand sport too well? Imagine: a group of men running around on a field, chasing the ball, running towards each other, running away, grabbing the ball and hurling it – and oneself – on to the ground, or throwing it to someone only to get it thrown back. And why do some people act in a certain way and not others? Why is *he* allowed to hold the ball, but *he* isn't? Why can *he* stand at the side and hold the ball and all the others line up?

Now imagine trying to explain it if both teams were wearing the same colours – or everyone wore different ones. And what if there were goal posts all the way round the field, and everyone had a different goal? Or if they seemed to be trying to kick the ball into one goal but then headed off to someone else's instead, or changed their minds about the rules half-way down the field? Or every now and then pulled out a knife and stabbed their opponent? Or they all wore blindfolds? How can you explain how *that* works?

And then, to complicate it further add twenty, or thirty women into the picture, playing a different game – with totally different rules. Or is it the same game but with different goals? You don't know. And what if they're all speaking different languages? Or maybe they're all speaking the same language – but the words have different meanings, depending who is saying them – or who they're saying them to.

Of course the women will pair up with the men now and then and run off the field with them to play a different game entirely. How does *that* fit into the overall game? And then suddenly there are children running in and out of the players' legs, grabbing the ball, falling over, crying, getting hurt. How do you explain the rules to them? It becomes a circus. Like life.

This book is a small attempt at explaining some of the basic rules. It gives the main ideas with necessarily broad brush strokes. We're all in there running for the goal. Or sitting on the sideline to watch now and then. We might play better if we had more idea of how the game works. The book won't explain how to manipulate people to make lots of money. Nor how to charm everyone to your point of view. Rather it is about learning to relate more openly and effectively – to lead a Good Life, with at least some members of the family close, and a few good friends. Maybe that's a goal worth running for.

In the game of life one of my big goals was a life-long marriage. But after twenty-five years the cracks got too big and my marriage fell apart. Some people berated me, 'As a counsellor and psychologist how can you do this? What hope is there for the rest of us? What's wrong with you?' What was wrong was that my most important relationship was not working. If our best learning is made from our mistakes I've been in a good learning place. I'm writing this book, not from having it all together, but from having learned from my mistakes along the way, still on the journey, still learning the rules. Still practicing to find how relationships work, experimenting and finding that some things I thought were rules don't work. Learning how to play the game of life. And experiencing the freedom of honesty – learning a little of what it means to be seen for who I am, and not hiding from the shame of my mistakes.

❶
Naked and Not Ashamed

Life after Eden

One of the most powerful stories in our Western psyche is that of the first man and the first woman. They lived in the Garden of Eden – the place of total happiness – they walked with their God and they were 'naked and not ashamed.' The story is telling us that we can relate to each other openly, and without shame or fear coming between us. However, ever since our beginnings, humankind has been in a lesser place, and we have lived with divisions between us, with shame. Shame for being less than we know we can be, shame for fear of not letting each other see who we truly are. What would it be like to have relationships where I could be naked, seen for who I am – and not ashamed? An impossible ideal – but still an ideal worth working towards, worth even the little glimpses of it we can achieve.

I remember as a teenager taking part in 'sensitivity training', learning some basic self-awareness and self disclosure – and the feeling of exultant freedom it brought. We are made for intimate relationships. There is a joy that results from openness, in being seen and accepted for who I am – 'warts and all.' The phrase 'warts and all' apparently came from Oliver Cromwell. His was the age of the cavaliers, of men wearing wigs and perfume. Important people had portraits painted to memorialize themselves. Of course the artist was usually smart enough to paint his subject in the best light, maybe with fewer wrinkles, and without any disfigurements. Oliver Cromwell was not an aristocrat, and he did have warts. He told his portraitist to paint him 'warts and all.' Most of us are not as brave as he was – at least not when it comes to our emotional world, our secret fears, our hidden shames and childhood wounds. In fact we defend ourselves far more than we even are able to admit to ourselves. It is a lifelong task to simply look at our own warts, let alone disclose them to others.

'Why am I afraid to tell you who I am?' asks John Powell[1] in his book of that name. And his answer is simple yet profound: because who I am is all I've got, and if you reject the real me, I have nothing else left. And so we wear masks to keep ourselves from shame, and as a result hide ourselves from ourselves, and even from those we love the most, for fear that if we are naked we will be thrown out of our Garden of Eden, even though at one level we know we no longer live there anyway. We grasp on to the illusion of our seeming lost paradise, the leftover pockets of Eden, hoping that we can be accepted and loved, but seldom letting go our fig leaves long enough to find out.

Trusting the seasons

For our relationships to work well, there has to be some risk-taking, some willingness to be vulnerable, to face the fear of rejection or shame. Usually risk-takers are those who have discovered that the pay-off is worth the price, those who are secure enough to risk some loss. The risk-takers are those who know that even though bad things happen, there is life on the other side. They understand that life goes through hard times, that winter is followed by spring, that if I hold on long enough times will change, summer will come again.

As I write I am sitting under the shade of a chestnut tree on a New Zealand summer day, with roses and pansies in the garden, and a willow catching the reflected shimmer of the stream beneath its branches. The blue sky highlights the green of trees and grass and garden. A summer's day in a country where the four seasons follow each other, not without variation – it's been the coldest December in sixty years – but still the seasons inevitably follow each other. Autumn will come and the willow and chestnut will turn yellow and their leaves will fall. Winter's tracery of twigs will pattern the grey winter sky, and cold southerlies will bring frost and snow. But then spring will come, the first crocuses even while the snow is still on the ground, and the snowdrops and freesias, irises and tulips, bringing colour and life after the brown and grey of winter. Each year I am reminded – there is loss and there is new life, there is death and there is birth, spring follows winter follows autumn. And I am reminded when the autumn winds start turning the leaves and stripping the trees, of Shelley's autumn ode, 'Oh wind, if winter comes can spring be far behind?' Why would I prefer these seasons to where I now live in subtropical Australia – where the seasonal changes are far less dramatic? Because part of me needs the reminder – winter will come, but so will spring. Death is part of life. Loss is part of living. But always there is hope. If I dare to let go of Eden, I can trust there is something better. If I risk losing the 'good' images of myself, I can trust that a more real, a more realistic self will emerge. Trusting that the rollercoaster ride of life, death, life will eventually indeed bring life.

What has all this to do with being naked and finding relationships? That the core of a relationship is risk-taking. Daring to let go of the fig leaves. Holding on to the belief that being known for who I am is worth risking the shame and the rejection. Daring to believe that being seen warts and all is better than hiding behind a mask. Relationships are formed out of trust – trust that the loss and pain is worth the ride. Trust that even though the winter of disconnection may come, spring and new life will return.

Try it

Think of one of your closest relationships, either in the past or the present.
What is it like when the other person sees your faults?
What about seeing their faults? – do you prefer the mask, not knowing who they are – or the reality?
What 'winters' have there been in the relationship?
How have you reconnected after a winter?

Learning to live the seasons

I have watched as babies begin this journey; the journey of learning that in relationships spring follows winter, and death is not the end. Research has been carried out – careful videos tracking the interaction between a baby and his caregiver. The child purses his lips, the parent copies, the baby makes a cooing sound, the parent imitates, the child sticks out his tongue, so does the adult – and so it goes on. Then the parent is distracted and looks away, the child continues his cooing, the parent ignores him. The child's sounds get louder and the parent responds again. A small winter has passed – a moment of loss, quickly followed by reconnection. The interaction continues, the parent is again busy, the child tries to call for attention, nothing happens. The child becomes distressed, begins to cry, the parent's attention returns, the baby is reassured. Life goes on.

So the interaction continues, so the relationship grows. In a healthy relationship the mother, the father, the caregiver, is not constantly available to the child, but he or she is always eventually available. The child learns that the universe is a safe place. Spring will follow winter. My basic needs will be met. There is pain and there is loss but I will not be left to die. I can eventually get attention, and can make the world respond to me, I can get my needs met, connection will be restored.

This most basic of relationships sets the pattern for later relationships. Unless I have a basic hope that connection will be restored, every loss is a final loss and life is a continual crisis. What we learned as a baby we continue to repeat in our relationships through childhood. We practice reconnecting after an interruption. We learn to make up after a fight. We dare to risk ourselves again in a relationship that is not continuously smooth. In early childhood years this basic connection can be represented by an inanimate object – a soft toy, a teddy bear, a security blanket. The soft warmth of the object reminds the child that human contact will return, that isolation is not death. While I am stating this in exaggerated terms, this is the reality of our deep inner experience, the terror of isolation or of death, which makes us cling inappropriately or grieve disproportionately. So all of childhood is a practicing of relationships, of finding who will remain steady, of learning how to keep an appropriate distance, of recognizing the signs of invitation to connect or reconnect.

Deeper dimensions

In adolescence we revisit our earlier learning. Our relationships have taken on new dimensions. On the one hand I am beginning to step out into the world as an adult – my relationships are not a given anymore, a natural and inevitable part of my family life. And on the other, sexuality and romance have added a deeper meaning to my relationships – a promise of ecstasy, a warning of agony. Again we practice the dance of loss and reconnection, some of us choosing isolation rather than risk the loss. Others choose many superficial relationships, keeping the masks in place. Or they relate only in certain safe contexts, sporting teams, classroom debate, situations where they are on a safe knowledge base. Or again they choose only prescribed roles, where they take on a role – whether a formal one: builder, secretary, mother, teacher; or an informal one: clown, expert, helper, rebel. A role where I do not risk telling you who I really am, so if you reject me you really only reject my role.

As an adolescent, a young adult, we learn the adult version of the dance of connection, of turning away or pulling back, of reconnection – of finding the appropriate distance for that particular relationship. If we have suffered wounds in our childhood years – and who hasn't? – or if we believe the media images of romance as being of life-and-death significance, we may find the danger and enticement of romantic/sexual relationships overwhelming. Many teenagers are caught by the illusion that romantic love is everything, that if I cannot be in love, life is hardly worth living, or that a romantic partner leaving me is the ultimate rejection. Finding a way through this particular winter can be a hugely challenging learning experience, but one which will eventually bear the fruit of self-acceptance if we can continue to seek reconnections with other people – not just the one we fell in love with.

This learning is essential if a long-term relationship is to work. Unless we can accept the small disconnections of everyday life we will cling possessively to our relationships, or be devastated by disagreements. We may think that the harmony of our major relationship is essential for survival. If we cannot disagree we will sacrifice our own sense of who we are, to please the other person. This is not true relationship – the relationship of two whole persons is sacrificed for seeming agreement. If my fear of disconnection is too strong then I sacrifice the relationship anyway because I am not a real person in that relationship.

Audrey had been one of three children, the youngest, with two older brothers. She had felt special being the only girl, even though her brothers teased her sometimes. Her mother was often busy with her work and her father was frequently away, but when he came home he would cuddle her and she would feel safe and happy. When she was around ten he started coming to her bed after she had fallen asleep, and so the sexual abuse began. Looking back she surmised that her parents were far from happy, and she realised her father had probably started drinking more and more. Through her teenage years she kept her distance from boys and began putting on weight. In her early twenties Audrey is trying to make sense of her ambivalence about men and her own sexuality. She is not even sure what is mask and what is reality. Or whether she even likes herself, let alone whether anyone else would like her.

As a young child Audrey had felt loved and accepted. She could ask for what she wanted, and apart from her brothers' reactions, mostly got it. She didn't have much experience in negotiation, and as a teenager was denied the practice of connection, disconnection and reconnection. There was no way she could deny her father, and she had nowhere to go to ask for help. She has not learned the necessary adult process of negotiating relationships at all.

The practice of negotiating relationships is meant to be part of the normal learning of the small child. The favourite word for a two year old is 'no'. While some overzealous parents may have thought this means their child is a born rebel, it is, rather, a normal part of the child learning that she is not just an extension of her mother. This is the beginning of awareness of boundaries. Childhood and adolescence should provide a loving, safe environment for us to practice boundaries – what is me, and what is not me, what the other person wants and what I want, how to get my needs met and how to respond to others' needs.

❷
Boundaries: Me and Not Me

In his autobiography, *Running with Scissors*,[2] Augusten Burroughs talks about his childhood relationships. The recent movie of the same name opens with a young Augusten putting curlers in his mother's hair. The voiceover says how much he loved his mother and how much she loved him. She is ringing the school to say Augusten won't be coming today. They laugh together as Augusten instructs her to tell the school he has put too much gel in his hair so he can't come. It becomes evident very quickly that while the child may indeed love his mother, she is totally self-absorbed and uses the relationship to meet her own needs for admiration and acceptance. Augusten thinks they have a loving relationship. It is obvious to the viewer that something is amiss – that it is a relationship of entanglement and enmeshment that will take Augusten many years, alcoholism, rehabilitation and therapy to work through. Somewhere along the way – maybe even before her child was born – Augusten's mother began to use her child to meet her own needs, rather than vice versa. She becomes a manipulative controller, not knowing her own boundaries, and certainly not helping her son find his. He eventually ran away to New York at fifteen to create a boundary between them.

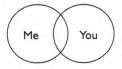

Clear boundaries between people

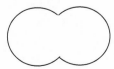

No boundary – what is me?

Childhood learning of boundaries

Fortunately most of us have an ordinary 'good-enough' mother –
a mother who is human and makes mistakes, but loves us enough
to help us grow to reasonably healthy adulthood. Before looking
further at boundary patterns we will review the usual development
of a child responding to and moving away from his primary caregiver – usually his mother.

In the womb the baby is physically joined to his mother with
the umbilical cord through which he receives nourishment, and
the beginning of the awareness of the mother's emotions. In a
sense he is one being with his mother. There is no separation,
what one hears the other hears, what one eats the other receives,
what one feels the other experiences. Then comes the separation
of birth. For many children physical closeness remains. The baby
is carried in a sling by one of the parents. He sleeps against his
parents' bodies, and he still receives nourishment from his mother's
body.

His eyes begin to see not just light and darkness, but shapes.
Especially he is attracted to the pattern of a face – two eyes and
a mouth. And when he drinks from his mother's breast the focal
length is just right to see his mother's eyes. He looks and turns
away and looks again. He begins to experiment with sounds and
hears the response. He begins to learn that he and his mother are
not one and the same being.

He practices this further, begins to crawl, to walk, to run away
from his mother. All this is healthy and good, the beginning of
learning that I am a person in my own right, I can make decisions
separately from my mother, I can choose not to come when she
calls. And still I am loved. The relationship may go through small
winters of disagreement but connection returns and I am still
loved. Love is not the same as control, and I am able to turn away.
A child who is controlled, who is not given some freedom, does
not learn well the lessons of these early years. That I am a separate
person. That I need other people. But I can still turn away, and
return, and be loved.

The two basic things a child – any of us – needs to learn are first, am I loved? and second, can I do whatever I like? For psychological health the answer to the first has to be yes. And to live in the real physical world and in relationships the answer to the second has to be no.

So the child experiments, pushing the boundaries, finding the yes's and no's, the disconnections and the reconnections, and survives the winter and the summer, and winter again. Somewhere around the end of the first year his experiments with sounds turn into words, and after another year of practice begin to become sentences. And all this while he has been learning the power of words, to get what he wants, to make people respond. Around two he discovers the power of the word 'no', and experiments with this word – that above all others – creates boundaries. The word that says most effectively 'I am not you, and I do not have to do what you want.' Or, 'I am not an object and I do not have to let you take my toys away.' Or, 'No, I will put my clothes on myself.' And so he becomes his own separate little person, if his parents will let her, and will continue to love him, and to teach him about the real world.

Life goes on. Relationships become more complicated, brothers and sisters, friends and classmates, relatives and neighbours become the context of his life. And in this interacting network he practices relationships, practices connecting and disconnecting, learns what behaviour gets him the love that he needs and the responses he seeks. And he practices boundary-setting, saying no, or deferring, or pushing to get his way.

A boundary – the line between us

A boundary is simply a line between two beings, two objects, two pieces of land. The line that says me and not-me, mine and not-mine. A line that divides what I am responsible for and can change, and what I am not responsible for and cannot change – at least not without violating what belongs to another. A boundary is as necessary as the fact that two people are two separate beings – somewhere a boundary line must exist.

Boundaries functioning correctly

Some years ago when I was learning about boundary keeping I experienced a clear demonstration of their importance. Some friends moved into a new house which had no fence. Their neighbours were a family of five children, and the mother was not well and let them run and play as they pleased. They came across the boundary line into my friends' property and into their house. My friends, trying to be kind and generous, and – with children of their own – allowed them to come. But the children would come and not go home. 'Children we are going to have dinner now,' – a usual signal to neighbours that it is time for them to leave. 'Oh that's okay,' the neighbour-children would say, 'we'll just stay and play with the toys.' They came and went as they pleased. And my friends, trying to be generous and helpful, let them. Until they couldn't stand it any more and lost their temper, and in reaction began to put some very clear no's in place. It was a summary lesson to me as an onlooker. I know in their place, I too would have bent over too far trying to be kind; not clarifying where the boundary of my own likes and dislikes lay, hoping that somehow the other person would work it out, until it became too pressing to ignore. It was a clear demonstration to me that relationships work best when boundaries are clear, when I state my preferences and let the other state theirs – and then find the distance at which the relationship will accommodate us both.

My friends eventually built a fence, and a gate, and set times when the neighbours' children could come. Boundaries are not castle walls – to keep others out at all costs. They are lines which state the edge of me, my preferences, my choices, my likes and dislikes. And there is a gate which lets others in, and times when I compromise to be in relationship with other people. Watching my friends helped me realise how much I live with invisible boundary lines – not saying what I want, trying to accommodate the other person, even at too much cost to myself. Every time I would teach boundary ideas, my marriage would go through a hiccup – as I reminded myself that it was better to state my preferences, to make my boundaries visible, rather than living as a contortionist in positions I could not maintain.

Try it

When do I find it most difficult to say no?
Are there times I feel resentful at others trespassing my boundaries?
Do I notice other people wanting to say no – and not doing it?
Does my partner have difficulty saying no?
Who has difficulty saying no to me?

It is easy to stereotype women as being the compliant, accommodating ones, and indeed that has been the modelling of previous generations. But stereotypes are less evident as men and women are given more freedom to 'be who they are'. Andrew would also be considered compliant. He has grown up in a secure family with two brothers. He is the middle child and the quietest. He tends to go along with what the others in his family want and has seldom found himself short of friends. He generally lets others make the decisions and is now getting established in his career, easygoing with his workmates and boss. When Andrew gets into a serious long term romantic relationship his lack of practice in stating his own needs will become an issue.

No – a basic boundary

Many of us are like Andrew, my friend and myself. Not wanting to say no, we put ourselves out to say yes, even beyond what we can continue to live with. We are the ones who have to learn to say no, to value our own selves enough to hold on to what is important to us. Many of us have come from families or cultures where we cannot really say no. Or only in subtle – or even manipulative – ways. And that is the outcome of not being able to say no. We say it in different ways. By withdrawing, ending the relationship, manipulating, making the other person pay in some way.

Even as I write at an outside table of a coffee shop, I hear a four-year-old boy practicing his boundaries; refusing to come when he is called, but then getting left behind; refusing to wheel his bike, but then grabbing it back when his father takes it; lagging behind so he doesn't seem to obey. If his parents can lovingly accept his practicing, he will learn how to say no appropriately, and how to say yes to fit in with others. If they reject him when he resists he will be caught in a world of winter, of having to make a choice between a sense of himself and staying connected. I cringe as the mother yells at him in anger and stalks off leaving him behind, and he ends up following her, crying. I hope that she will learn to give him space to practice and yet let him know he is loved unconditionally.

I think of my children at that age. I so wanted them to know that my love would always be there. I remember saying to my three-year-old son, 'Do you know that I love you, that whatever you do, I'll still love you?' His eyes went wide – 'No, I didn't know that.' A year or two later, I asked him the same question. He looked at me as though I was a bit slow. 'Yes, I know that!'

Saying no, hearing no

For healthy relationships we need a strong basic acceptance, and we need to learn to make our boundary lines visible. For some of us that first means identifying what we want. We have so practiced compliance that we give to others what they want continually, not wanting to rock the boat, thinking we are being more loving by doing only what others want. Irenaeus of the second century CE said 'The glory of God is a person fully alive.' Continually deferring to others is not being fully alive, not knowing who I am and what I want. Relationships will always entail compromise, but knowing what I want and choosing to put it aside for love of another person is a very different dynamic than simply deferring constantly without ever knowing who I am and what I prefer. Authenticity is being able to express myself, to live what I am, both inside and out.

While some of us have chosen compliance as our major relationship strategy, others – controllers – have chosen to state strongly what they want. While the compliant ones of us are not good at saying no, there are those, usually extroverts, who are not good at *hearing* no. They have practiced identifying what they want, stating it, and getting it – and not listening too much to what others say so they don't hear their disagreement. Of course these two kinds of people often attract each other. The more controlling one says what they want, and the more compliant one goes along with it. And it works reasonably for a time. But this is not a healthy relationship, merely an affiliation.

While the compliant ones of us cannot say no, the controllers cannot hear no. They may have grabbed hold of life more obviously, identified what they want more explicitly, but they often sacrifice relationships because they do not hear the preferences or needs of the compliants with whom they are trying to be in relationship. Some people are obvious extrovert controllers. They state what they want often and loudly. They demand to be heard. They cut across what others say. The fact is that most of us go along with a clearly stated preference – but then we may withdraw from the relationship, not even giving feedback to the controller that their behaviour has offended us. And the controller finds himself without friends as a result.

Julie is a sales representative in the computer industry. She was the oldest of four children and often looked after the little ones. Through school she was often chosen to be a leader of sports teams or interschool competitions and was recognized as an all-round achiever. She's had a number of romantic relationships but none that last long. 'I say it as I see it,' she says. 'I'm beginning to think men just can't handle a woman who knows her own mind.'

Lately though, she has been attending some training courses and learning about different approaches to different personality types. She's begun to wonder if what she had considered forthrightness might not be seen as abrasive or even controlling. She's always thought it is better to say what you mean rather than beat about the bush. In fact the other group of people who are considered controllers particularly irritate Julie.

The other kind of controllers are more subtle than Julie is. In many cultures, women are not given much permission to be outright controllers, so they learn more subtle ways of control. They simply don't cooperate. Or they are sick when others make the decision they don't want, or tired, or upset, or withdrawn. They make it uncomfortable for those who don't go along with what they want. Or they manipulate more explicitly, 'I'd be so disappointed if you didn't come to my place'; 'I'm so tired after all the cooking I've done'; 'I was really hoping we could all be together';'After all these years I would have thought this once we might…'; and so on.

The mark of the controller is that they don't give freedom to the other person to say what they want. They push for what they want, and don't hear the no of the other person. Julie had learned through her school years to say what she wanted. Indeed, this characteristic had been praised as a 'leadership quality.' But she had not practiced listening to what other people wanted. All of us learn strategies to try and get what we want, to get the love we want, but often, as Julie is discovering, we might sacrifice a real relationship in the process. The compliants are afraid to go through the winter of the other person's displeasure for fear that their will be no spring. Or, if we are controllers, we do not give into what the other person wants for fear we cannot have what we want. A real relationship needs seasons to be healthy. Indeed, a real relationship risks loss and isolation in order to safeguard the authenticity of each person.

Of course, it's not as simple as this may imply. We may be compliants most of the time but controllers in certain relationships – or vice versa. Or we may opt for manipulative control if outright statement of preference doesn't work. The point is that we need to learn how to be assertive, to state what we want, to listen to the other, and then to negotiate rather than bulldozing over the other person, or lying down and letting the other have what they want at my cost.

All of us will have a 'default' pattern – a pattern we tend to go to, a habitual response to others which we practice without thinking. It is useful to be aware of the patterns that people choose, the 'games' we play in order to become more free in our choices and responses to those we relate to.

Try it

Are there people in your life who you can see are controllers?
Do they tend to be direct, pushy, or manipulative?
What is it like for you when you feel someone is being controlling?
In which relationship do you tend to be the controller?
Do you use direct control, or are you more manipulative?

Default patterns

There are four main default patterns of boundaries.[3] Controlling and complying are the two most obvious patterns. The other two are less obvious – and are sometimes linked with the first two. Complying, not being able to say no, is often accompanied by not being able to *hear* yes. I will do what you want, go along with your preferences, but I don't expect anyone to help *me* – resist it even. 'Oh no dear, I'm all right, don't go out of your way for me.' Compliants have put so much energy into saying yes to everyone else that they often can't accept people saying yes to them. They find it uncomfortable, even confrontational. These are the avoidants. They can't hear yes, can't receive the service of others.

	No	Yes
Can't say	**Compliants** Can't say no	**Non-responsive** Can't say yes
Can't hear	**Controllers** (Outright or Manipulative) Can't hear no	**Avoidants** Can't hear yes

The fourth kind of boundary difficulty is that of not being able to *say* yes. This is often people who have so learned to look after 'number one' that they do not know how to reach out to other people. They do not respond to the needs around them, sometimes they simply do not see them. Their relationships are thus very limited because there is seldom initiative, or even response to what others want. Their relationships tend to be built around what they want, and in this sense are quite immature – not having faced the childhood lesson of learning that 'I cannot have everything I want.' Or they tend to live in isolation, not knowing how to reach out to others, to listen for their preferences.

Sometimes this pattern is linked to that of the controller, pushing for 'what I want', and choosing not to say yes to what others want.

Family interactions forming boundaries

It is not difficult to imagine some of the childhood dynamics which may have set people up to default to these boundaries patterns. Children with authoritarian parents tend to learn to comply. They know that they must do what they're told, that in a way they 'can't say no', they must obey. This is especially true if fear is bound up in the relationship – the child learns not only to do what she is told, but what is implied, or what she guesses the authority figure wants. She learns a pattern of compliance, which becomes an inner part of who she is, even when she moves into relationships with people who do not expect this.

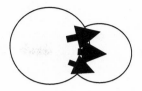

Controller   Compliant

In contrast, a child who grows up in a family where she doesn't get anything unless she fights for it, or at least makes her needs felt, learns to be a controller. It may even be that at home with a strong father, or a strong mother, she acted compliantly, but once out in the world she copies the patterns of the dominant parent and makes them her patterns. Controlling behaviour obviously gets us what we want – at least in the short term. But it is not a good pattern for ongoing intimate relationships.

Different children in the same family respond differently to family interactions. One child in a family may be more sensitive than others, may feel conflict almost as physical pain. It is unlikely that this child is going to become a controller, even the more subtle manipulative controller. It is more likely that she will withdraw, developing an avoidant pattern, or a non-responsive pattern, where she shields herself from the needs of others.

An even more challenging environment in which to grow up is one where parents are fickle about boundaries, sometimes letting the child demand anything and at other times punishing them for the slightest expression of need. Alcoholic or addicted parents are prone to this kind of erratic behaviour, which creates instability for the child, who in response may learn over-compliance, or total withdrawal – or in contrast, as she gets older, a controlling pattern, taking on the authority the parent used so poorly.

An even worse result of childhood trauma can be 'reverse' boundary keeping. Boundaries are necessary to protect us, to keep us healthy, to keep the good in and the bad out. Our skin is the most obvious boundary, keeping our internal organs safe inside and keeping out unhealthy viruses or diseases. A reverse boundary is one that keeps the good out and the bad in. Children who have suffered trauma, or who have been abused, often feel as though they are bad. Somehow an internal justice system makes us think, as children, that we get what we deserve, so traumatic events, especially abuse by those close to us, sows the lie that we are bad and deserve only badness. As a result children of these circumstances use their boundaries to keep the bad in and the good out.

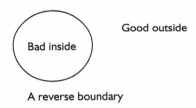

A reverse boundary

They do not receive the good things that are said to them, they do not trust the love that may be extended. In adult life they still tend to think of themselves as bad or undeserving and interpret their relationships as confirming this belief.

It is not just the family dynamic that forms the boundary patterns in children. We are born with at least some parts of our temperament, for example, a tendency to extraversion or introversion. There is an interaction of these inborn characteristics with our childhood environment and the family dynamics and other environmental factors have a great impact. The fact that children in the same family are very different points to the complexity of the interactions.

Many of us have not realized that good boundaries are necessary for healthy relationships. We may have even thought that our relationships were particularly loving because we are so responsive to others' needs. Or that our family is close because we 'know' what the other person 'needs' without them saying so. Or that we are leaders, always letting others know what is the best outcome, not realizing that we are pushing people around in the process. How do we know what we should communicate to others, and what we should keep to ourselves? How do we know when to press the other to change, or let them know their behaviour offends us?

Of course, there are no easy answers. Relationships are complex. People are sensitive – or insensitive – and often we do not know what is under the surface. Or we know all too clearly, and know to keep our distance. It is however worth exploring what is within our boundaries, and what is not, what I am responsible for and what is the other person's responsibility.

Inside my boundaries

The example of my friends' fence line was an obvious example of a concrete boundary, a line showing the edge of the property. This is my property. I am responsible for maintaining it and looking after it, and I have the right to say who comes across the line and when. If there were no property marker I would not know which plants I could take out, which lawn I was responsible to mow. Similarly, objects in my possession are my responsibility – and I have the right to lend them to whom I please, and to expect them to be returned.

In some cultures, where people have far less clear rules about possession, everything belongs to everyone. Or the land belongs to us all. In some ways this may look idyllic to those of us looking on from the outside. And it may indeed be a more free way to live, or a more responsible one. The point is that for relationships to work we need to have societal agreement about possession, ownership, property, land. It may well be that the Australian aboriginal holding of the land as sacred – and therefore everybody's responsibility – produced much better environmental care. Or it may only work in a society where beliefs and lifestyle fitted with a nomadic, simpler way of being. Either way, everyone had to agree on where the boundaries were, and who the responsibilities belonged to.

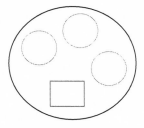

Me and my possessions   Us and our possessions

For some years my family lived in a community. Sharing general possessions made a lot of sense. We didn't have to all buy washing-machines, lawnmowers or cars; we could share. It was a much more people-friendly and environmentally friendly arrangement. But generally people understood that appliances were not looked after so well – because they weren't actually 'mine.' When the lawnmower got burnt one day because of the ignorance of one person, who then was responsible for replacing it?

Eventually we too moved to suburbia and bought our own individual appliances. I still wish I could live in the idealism and challenge of those early days. Challenge because owning things in common forces us to voice our frustrations, and our preferences about the joint possessions. Whatever arrangement we live by – whether sharing possessions, or each having our own for which we are responsible – we have to have agreement about boundaries, and this tells us who is responsible for what.

It is easier to clarify who owns which possessions, and who owns what land. But what about attitudes, beliefs, feelings, decisions? When we are small children we generally 'inherit' the beliefs and attitudes of our parents. As we become teenagers we hopefully work out our own. But herein lies a difficulty. At what point do my religious beliefs become my own, for example? Different families and different cultures work this out differently. Some families insist their children attend church with them until they leave the family home. In some religions a change of belief is punishable by death. Or there are far more subtle pressures. Inferences that one person is a black sheep, or a lost soul, or on his way to hell, if he believes differently from the rest of the family. Or rather if he dares to give voice to, or to live out, that belief. And many families would not realise that this is a boundary issue. When we begin to *name* boundaries, what is mine and what is not mine, then it is a lot easier to identify my beliefs and my attitudes as my own – my responsibility and my freedom of choice. I can then recognize pressure to change as just that, rather than feeling guilty that I see things differently, or having to hide my beliefs, attitudes or values.

My behaviour, my responsibility

My own behaviour is more clearly within my boundaries, and I am responsible for it. At first thought this might seem obvious – I am responsible for looking after myself, eating enough food, doing the work expected of me. I am responsible for what I do, the way I act. But it becomes more complicated. Am I responsible for what I say? For what I don't say? If I do not speak up when I see someone doing something wrong, am I complicit? Being responsible for my own behaviour is actually rather complex. How many times have I said 'But she made me do it!'; 'The teacher said we had to!'; or, more subtle, 'But everyone does it.'

If I cheat on my income tax because 'everyone does it', am I responsible for my behaviour? If I waste resources, and do not recycle, am I responsible for the state of the environment? If I do nothing to prevent babies dying of starvation, because they are away in another country, am I responsible for their deaths? The boundary lines become complex.

The main point is that *I* am responsible for *my* behaviour. And if I use the excuse that someone else 'made' me do it, I am giving away agency – I am giving away the freedom to choose my own behaviour to the whims and choices of someone I make more powerful than myself. Our language will often give us clues when we are doing this – 'I had to…'; 'She made me…'; 'I didn't want to but…' Even the use of shoulds is an indicator of giving away my choice and freedom. 'I should,' 'I had to.'

Try it

Try and notice when you use the language of shoulds. Sometimes it's easier to notice it in other people's words first, as our own have become so habitual.

When you catch yourself saying 'should' or 'have to', try replacing it with the words, 'I am choosing to,' or 'I am making this a priority because...'

Looking for a reason for choosing to act this way gives clues to our values, and what, or who, we are giving power to – and as a result helps us to be more in control of our lives.

Learning to recognize boundaries calls us into adulthood. Taking responsibility for my actions, my words, my beliefs, values and attitudes brings about maturity more than just about anything else. I can stay a child and blame others for the way I am, what I believe, the way I behave; or I can claim adulthood and the freedom and responsibility that are part of it. One of the most demanding elements of being an adult is recognizing and taking responsibility for my own feelings.

3
Owning My Own Feelings

Learning the boundaries of possessions, behaviour and beliefs is complicated enough but a more subtle and more fraught area of entanglement in relationships is feelings. It seems that we have to learn explicitly to 'own our own feelings' or we will consider other people responsible for our feelings, or else feel responsible for theirs. 'You make me so angry'; 'You've made me so sad'; 'You've spoilt my day'; are all statements that give away agency, that is, they try and make someone else responsible for my feelings. Or, in contrast, 'Now I've made you sad'; 'I'm so sorry I made you angry'. One of the basic lessons in counselling training – or any basic communication course – is how to own our own feelings, to take responsibility for what I feel and not blame anyone else.

Feelings – inside my boundaries
Tom was talking about the conflict he is having with his wife. 'But she makes me so angry. If she didn't say the things she does, I wouldn't get angry.' His was a typical understanding that his feelings are really someone else's responsibility – as if his wife is holding the strings to his emotions. It is quite a challenge to learn to say, 'I am angry.' We may need to add, 'I get angry when you snap at me like that.' The important thing is that I acknowledge that my anger is my own – it is my feeling and I am responsible for it. Someone else in my position may not get angry, however much my wife snapped at them. That is because they are not so emotionally invested in the relationship, and do not have the history of the relationship. Nevertheless it is not the wife who is controlling the anger. If I can learn to own it as mine, then I can also experience the freedom of being able to change, and

being able to feel differently. The challenge is to use 'I' statements – 'I am angry,' 'I am hurt,' 'I am disappointed,' rather than 'you' statements.

For most of us this is an area of difficulty – and an invitation to maturity. It *feels* as though what the other person does makes me feel a certain way. If my partner says something critical I feel hurt, if my father disapproves of what I am doing I feel guilty, or judged, or rebellious. If they accept me I feel satisfied. There is no question that other people's behaviour, words and attitudes influence how we feel – especially people who are close to us, or people we look up to. Nevertheless my feelings are my own and I can learn to respond differently.

Those people who we admire, our heroes, are often people who are able to own their own feelings – who can respond with courage in the face of rejection, who can respond with love in the face of hatred. Almost always these are men and women who have done the hard work of owning their own emotions, taking responsibility for their own reactions and choosing how they will respond however the other behaves.

Nelson Mandela did not have to go to jail. He could have appealed the judge's decision. But he decided to accept whatever decision the judge made, even the death sentence, because he believed that the law was unjust and needed to be changed, and the way to change it was to suffer the consequences of its existence.[4] He could have become a hard and bitter man. He chose to forgive. We admire him because we recognize that he chose not to allow his enemies to dictate what he would feel. We respect Martin Luther King because he chose not to be bitter against his racist countryman, but worked over and over to encourage his African-American peers to forgive and work for a better future. We admire Mother Teresa for her work amongst the destitute and dying in Calcutta, overcoming a natural feeling of revulsion, to care for them as she would a loved one.

We also differentiate between people who choose their responses of courage and forgiveness, and those who we see as merely being walked over, afraid to stand up for what is right, denying their feelings of anger or hurt. We do not respect those who are simply walked over. What we aspire to is that ability to feel the emotions, but choose our responses, guided by our values. It is hard work to take responsibility for our feelings and respond from a place of freedom. It often takes years of acknowledging the reality of our feelings but responding out of a choice to love or forgive or challenge.

Another reason many of us struggle with owning our own feelings is that we need practice in recognizing and naming them. We are more comfortable with talking about our thoughts. Acknowledging our feelings causes us to feel vulnerable or uncomfortable. Some of us *think* we are acknowledging our feelings when we are really still in our heads. I remember having it pointed out to me that I was saying 'I feel *that*...' As soon as we add 'that' we are really talking about what we think, or we are using a sneaky way to blame the other person. 'I feel that you are accusing me'; 'I feel that this is all a smokescreen.' Both these statements are what I *think*. If I am to be honest I need to name the feeling: 'I feel hurt, because you seem to be accusing me'; 'I feel frustrated because we are not talking about the real issue.'

Owning my own feelings and admitting them goes a long way towards resolving the issues between people. Realizing that the other person is hurt can often make all the difference in my response of compassion and willingness to negotiate. Acknowledging my own anger can free me to make the changes I need to make.

Strong emotions

The power of emotion is complicated further by the relationships the feelings are connected with. Our feelings are often so entangled in a relationship, in the presence of another person. Romantic relationships are particularly vulnerable to transfer or projection of feeling on to the other person. When I am in love it is very difficult to see the other person objectively – to believe that he is not also in love with me, or that he is not deliberately hurting me. Somehow the volume of emotion is turned up to its highest level

and owning the feelings that are mine is especially demanding. It
feels as though the other person is responsible for what is happening
to me. It feels as though they should make *me*, and how I feel, their
top priority. Romantic songs – and website blogs – are full of this
kind of language and projection. 'I am in love with you – how can
you be so *cruel* as to reject me?' 'I will die if you do not return my
love.' 'I love you and I need you as part of my life.'

Pain also causes us to project the responsibility of our feelings
on to other people. 'I am hurting so badly that you should...'
If the other person only knows how bad it is for me, they will
have to do what I want. It isn't that we are necessarily trying
to manipulate the other person. It is just that the feeling is so
overpowering it *feels* as though they should have to respond to me.
The learning of becoming a separate adult person – individuation
– is the acceptance that my feelings are my own, and my life is my
own, and no-one else is responsible for me – nor I for them. They
can choose to respond. I can choose to respond to them. But the
choices are free choices, and the strength of my feelings makes no
difference – except for me to acknowledge them.

Each one of us needs to learn to become a separate self and to
release others to be separate selves also. C. Day Lewis, the twentieth-
century British Poet Laureate, expressed it thus; 'Selfhood begins
with a walking away, and love is proved in the letting go.'[5] True love
is not clinging, however much romantic love tears our hearts. And
I am not responsible for fixing anybody else's emotions, however
deeply they are hurting. These are hard lessons for those of us who
have strong emotions, and those of us who are in pain or in the
ecstasy of romantic love.

Audrey, who was sexually abused as a child, finds owning her
own feelings particularly difficult. Her father forcing her to
comply, her own responses of wanting to please him, her hidden
hurt and anger, have made it very difficult for her to know what is
'hers' and what is really 'his'. Her boundaries have been so violated
that she finds her own feelings suspect, her need for acceptance
overwhelming. Her compliance with others' feelings in order to
get her needs met causes her to hide her feelings from herself.

All of us need practice in identifying our feelings – and in knowing what is mine and what is not mine. The practice and the naming bring freedom and maturity.

The root word of emotion is motion, movement, energy. Emotions are meant to motivate us, to give us energy. When we do not own them or acknowledge them we are repressing the energy, or giving the agency – the power – to the other person. When I admit my anger, there is the energy to bring about change. When I state my hurt, I am able to respond more freely. Many people who are 'depressed' are in fact de-pressing their emotion, pressing it down, hiding it from themselves. It takes more energy to press down our emotions and we are left tired, flat, without energy – depressed. Many people who are learning to own their own feelings, to acknowledge their anger, hurt or pain, find they have more energy. Their depression is an invitation to feel, to find the energy hidden below the surface.

Try it:

Think over the last week. Try and name as many different emotions you have experienced during the week. I felt... angry, hurt, disappointed, afraid, rejected, irritated, happy, misunderstood, anxious, judged, encouraged, sad, annoyed, lonely, elated. Over the next few days practice noticing how you feel. Name the emotion itself.

If you can, you may want to add a 'because' phrase – but be careful that this does not become a giving away of ownership of the feeling. This is my feeling – I am feeling it, no-one else has made me feel it.

As we become more adept at noticing our feelings we may recognize another subtle aspect of owning our feelings. Most of us judge our feelings as good or bad. The 'happy' feelings are 'good', the others 'bad'. Anger, in particular, usually gets labelled as bad. But anger is a great source of energy. Anger is usually the result of hurt, rejection or injustice, or maybe fear. Anger energizes us to do something about the catalyst – the injustice, the wounding, the cause of the fear. If we refrain from labelling the emotion as good or bad we can tap into the energy that comes with it. Certainly anger very often leads us to do something we feel badly about afterwards – but that is because we have not learned to channel it well. No emotion is good or bad in itself. It is simply an indicator of something else, a response to the environment, a response to other people and my perception of them. Emotions are the most effective doorway into knowing ourselves – and thus other people.

Feelings linked to beliefs

A story I heard can serve to illustrate that our feelings are always responses to something or someone else, and our perceptions of that. Mrs Jones went into hospital for a fairly routine and straightforward operation. When she was ready to come home the nurse would ring her daughter, Mrs Smith, to come and pick her up from the hospital. Sure enough, in the middle of the afternoon Mrs Smith got a call from the hospital. But it was not what she was expecting.

'Is that Mrs Smith?'

'Yes.'

'Mrs Smith, your mother, Mrs Jones, had an operation today.'

'Yes, that's right.'

'Mrs Smith, I am wondering if you have someone with you right now?'

'Well yes I do as a matter of fact, my neighbour is here. But why are you asking me that?'

'I'm so sorry to have to tell you this, but the operation was not a success. I'm wondering if you would like to come in and speak with the doctor.'

'What do you mean, not a success? Tell me what you are saying.'

'I'm so sorry Mrs Smith, but your mother has not survived the operation.'

Of course the daughter is shocked, in grief, angry, confused. She calls her husband asking him to come home and go to the hospital with her. She calls a close friend, and in tears tells her what has happened. Before her husband arrives, however, the phone rings again. It's the hospital.

'Is that Mrs Smith?'

'Yes.'

'Mrs Smith, was it your mother, Mrs Jones, who had an operation today, with Dr Jackson?'

'Yes, that's right.'

'Well, I just want to apologize for what has happened. There has been a mix-up. There was another Mrs Jones, with a daughter Mrs Smith, but her operation was with a different doctor. I'm afraid someone got the names confused. Your mother is just fine and you can come and pick her up now.'

However unlikely the story, the point is that Mrs Smith felt very real grief, pain and anger. Her feelings were real. Her *belief* that her mother had died was what was in error. Our feelings are responses to what we *believe* about a situation – not the situation itself. It *feels* as though our emotions are a response to reality – but they are always a response to our perception of reality. And our perception is shaped by previous history, earlier similar events, interpretations of the meaning of what has happened.

When Tom gets angry with his wife it is because she has behaved like this so many times before. And she *knows* he is hurt when she snaps at him. She *knows* it makes him angry and she shouldn't do it. And she is behaving *just* like his mother used to when he couldn't do everything she wanted. So his perception fuels his anger. Someone else sitting in his chair does not react in anger because they do not have the same history or the same relationship – and therefore they do not have the same perception. Even believing that my wife is responsible for my anger is a perception which results in me being more angry. My beliefs, my perceptions and interpretations are the origin of the emotion.

This is the basic foundation of cognitive behavioural therapy, CBT. Our emotions, our problems – whatever has caused us to seek help – are linked to our thoughts, our cognitions. If we are willing to examine our thoughts, and find where they are faulty, we will be able to experience different emotions, and our problems will be solved. Mrs Smith's problems were solved as soon as the faulty belief that her mother had died was corrected. Obviously our faulty beliefs are not as easily corrected as in this example, but nevertheless uncovering our beliefs and perceptions can be powerful in changing our experience of what we feel.

If we are to own our own feelings, it is often helpful to understand why they are so powerful, or what the beliefs are that have made the feeling so strong. Often the beliefs that inject the most power into our feelings are black-and-white thinking or exaggerated beliefs. In the example of Tom above, it may well be that his anger relates to black-and-white thinking about his wife's behaviour. 'She is *never* going to listen to me,' or 'She is *just* like my mother, and my parents' marriage broke up so mine will too.' If I believe my wife is snapping at me because she is under pressure with the baby crying, and the pot on the stove boiling over, but she will be fine after dinner; that is a very different experience from the belief that her snapping means my marriage is almost over, and my life is devastated. I can respond to her in compassion rather than anger and hurt, depending on my beliefs about her behaviour. Our beliefs make all the difference to our feelings.

Anger

Anger is perhaps the most difficult emotion to own, and to process well. This may be because it is always about something else – psychologists call it a secondary emotion – it is a response to something else that comes first. Whether this something else is a belief, as explored in the section above, or whether it is a reaction to some other feeling, it is 'secondary' to that belief or feeling. Usually anger is about injustice, pain, loss or powerlessness. Often it is about a boundary violation.

One of the complications of anger is that many of us have been taught to repress it – or we have had repression of anger modelled to us. We are hardly aware that we are angry and have difficulty being able to admit it; sometimes we can only identify ourselves as being 'irritated' or 'frustrated'. Complicating it further is the guilt that many of us associate with being angry. We think that feeling angry is wrong – but no emotion is wrong. An emotion is simply an indicator of a reaction – an action can be wrong, but not a feeling. Our first learning task is to notice when we are angry, even if it is only irritation or frustration.

Some of us have had the opposite experience – we have grown up in families where there is explosive, even violent, anger. As a result we either copy this, believing it will 'clear the air' or we vow never to be like that, falling into the repression trap instead.

Try it

When did you last get angry/ irritated/ frustrated? Did you express your anger? How?
Was there a destructive element to the expression of anger?
In your childhood, how did each member of your family express anger?
What was it like for you when you experienced others' anger?
If you have a partner how does he/she express anger? What is that like for you?

Anger is often such a powerful emotion that we may have difficulty knowing where it rightly belongs. The first step is to identify what the anger is about, to be able to complete the sentence, 'I am angry (irritated/frustrated) because…'. Part of identifying what the anger is about may be to name the loss, injustice or hurt. Often there is an expectation that has not been met or a boundary that has been crossed. This should be identified also. To deal with anger constructively I need to be able to say 'I am angry because she is late again. I had particularly asked her to be on time and I feel disappointed and let down. I'm left thinking that she really doesn't respect me and what is important to me is not important to her.'

Part of naming the reason for my anger is to be specific about it. Anger often spreads to other people or from other occasions. I can be angry at my girlfriend because 'she is late and my mother was *always* late, and you just can't *trust* women *at all*.' In other words, the frustrations and hurts of other relationships and other occasions easily leach into the present frustration, fuelling my anger and hurt. And then my anger spreads and infects other unrelated relationships – all women, all bosses, all bank tellers. Or I may be angry with my boss but not dare to express it, so it comes out in my frustration with my partner – or vice versa. Often, people who are learning how to be angry will swing to an opposite extreme and express anger inappropriately for a time.

Another reason for naming my anger then is to notice where it belongs, and where it doesn't belong – so that my response can be appropriate. The idea of counting to ten when we are angry is to allow the first flash of adrenaline to lessen so that I can think clearly enough to be appropriate. Anger is a wonderful motivator but it is like a powerful motor which I need to learn to drive well.

The questions, 'What is this anger about?'; 'What has caused it?'; 'Who is it about?' can be followed by 'Where has a boundary been crossed?' and therefore 'What is my responsibility here?' The energy of anger can help us to address its real cause – whether it is in myself or in someone else. The anger may really be about my own procrastination, or unwillingness to address an issue. In this case the energy of the anger may help me make a change. Or it may be about a boundary violation which does show a lack of respect – or even awareness – of the other person. In that case the anger can give me the energy to bring out the issue into the open.

Here of course is delicate ground. I need to own my own anger, I need to approach the other person from an 'on-side' position (more on that later), speak assertively (more on that too), and if possible I should suggest a constructive solution. 'I'm feeling really angry because I've had to wait for half an hour. I know that being on time is hard for you. I'm wondering if in future you could text me when you are ready and I'll let you know how soon I can be there.' 'I'm angry because you said you would definitely have this report finished by today. I know you've had a lot of things on your plate. Perhaps in future we could check in a couple of days before and see if you need help to finish it.'

Sometimes we cannot find a solution and may need the other person to help. 'I'm angry because we had agreed that you would bring the children to my place, and now again you're saying you need me to come and get them. Can we make a time to sit down and work out an arrangement that is going to work for both of us.' Or we may need a third party to help us talk constructively to find a solution. Even someone who will sit in silence can be helpful to keep us rational in interactions which otherwise could flash into anger or destructiveness.

Defusing amplified emotions

Our experience of anger and beliefs about how to express it – as well as the beliefs we are reacting to – have a powerful effect on our actions. Similarly, our cultural beliefs about romance, and about the emotional pain which accompanies romantic relationship break-ups, add huge weight to our feelings about our partner. During teenage years most adolescents learn about male–female relationships by 'going out with' various partners. They learn the patterns of connecting, disconnecting and reconnecting in the context of romantic love. If their beliefs are that this is a time of learning, of being with someone in a respectful way for a short time to learn who they get along with most easily, and to learn how the give and take of relationships work, then a relationship will not be so devastating when it breaks up. However, if they believe that they need a romantic partner to make life worth living, that if the person they are with now decided not to live with them forever or decided not to be in love with them, then life is over – of course they will feel desperately rejected if their partner leaves. If I have been taught by the culture of my peers that 'I will die without your love', then withdrawal of love conjures up feelings of facing death.

Albert Ellis, who pioneered therapy which addressed our hidden beliefs underlying our actions and reactions, often worded beliefs humourously to expose their exaggeration. For example, 'One absolutely must be competent, adequate and achieving in all important respects or else one is an inadequate, worthless person.' He called this process 'awfulizing' to show how we overstress the idea. Often simply recognizing the amplification and rewording the belief is sufficient to help us react more appropriately. 'It is true that I did not complete that task very well – but I am still learning and no-one else expects me to be competent yet. Anyway being incompetent does not make me worthless – I am still a valuable, lovable person.'

Any thoughts that have extreme words will feed into the pattern of awfulizing. 'Always' and 'never' are common ways to fuel an emotion. He *never* listens. It will *always* be like this. I *must* get it right or *everyone* will *hate* me.

Try it

Think over the week and identify a strong emotion (or any emotion, if you are someone who doesn't allow yourself strong emotions). Try to say the words of your underlying belief. State the emotion – 'I was angry/hurting/scared because (state what it is about) and I believe that therefore…'. Try to fill in the blank. Especially try to state it in the strongest terms you need to, to match the strength of your emotion.

Over the next few days, continue to repeat the process as you notice your feelings.

Recognizing the beliefs or perceptions that are fuelling our emotions can help us to recognize that these are indeed *my* emotions; I can own them.

Mindfulness

Identifying the faulty beliefs that inflate our emotions is an important way of defusing the power of our emotions and therefore our overreactions to other people. Another important way of working with our emotions is learning how to stop them becoming obsessions. Our brain is wired in such a way that our thought patterns form habitual neurological links. I start a thought… and the tape runs on by itself. The unbidden thoughts or memories link to my thought or feeling and the same scenario or reaction plays over and over. This only strengthens the brain's neural connections and I set an automatic pathway of cognition and accompanying emotion – or heightening emotion, as the case may be.

Audrey's thought patterns around men go something like this: 'That man is looking at me. All men want the same thing. He won't want a relationship with me though. No-one ever likes me after the first date. I'm never going to be able to get married. I'm just useless.' Thus her 'tape' of thought patterns plays over, and she is left feeling hopeless and lonely. She needs a way to break the chain of linked thoughts and emotions. She may find that mindfulness helps.

An increasing amount of research is being done on practices of mindfulness – 'meditation', or 'centring prayer', depending on one's spirituality. Mindfulness is the practice of staying in the present. An example is the simple practice of sitting quietly with eyes closed and centring on one phrase, picture or prayer. Naturally our thoughts will wander, but we then gently bring them back to our chosen phrase or word. Our thoughts wander again and again. Some people call this the monkey mind – this incessant chatter that we all have in our heads. Many of us have thought that this endless noise is an inescapable part of life, but meditation practices help us to still them. One's religious affiliation will inform the word or phrase that one chooses – the important thing is to choose something which helps me relax, let go of the babble and sit in stillness.

It is important that I am very patient with myself here. All of us will tend to return to the babble, the incessant chatter, the obsessive thoughts or feelings, but that is the point of the exercise – that I am practicing letting go. I am weakening the power these thoughts have over me, lessening the grip of the reactionary emotions. As I notice that my thoughts have wandered off again in the same old pattern, I simply use that recognition to come back to the centre again. I am giving my brain new pathways, a new habit pattern of stillness and agency.

Research is already showing that mindfulness practices are powerful in keeping addicts from returning to their addictions. In a sense, we are all addicts. We all have over-indulgences that we turn to when we are not wanting to face the pain and frustration of life. Some of us have obvious addictions – alcohol, smoking, drugs, sex, TV. Others may be more subtle – shopping, exercise, eating, surfing the Internet, arguing. Whatever it is that I turn to when I am hurt, bored or lonely can become an addiction because I am using it to cover the hurt instead of dealing with the hurt constructively.

Mindfulness exercises give our brains a different way of freeing ourselves from emotional reactions, or from the obsessive thoughts associated with them. It is important that I am patient with myself about the babble, or about finding my thoughts far away from where I was trying to be. If I criticize myself for doing badly I only increase the negative patterns. Being kind to myself, returning gently to my centring word, is a way of teaching my brain stillness.

The teachers of mindfulness suggest we sit in silence for twenty minutes at least once a day. Probably most of us spend that much time obsessing, or indulging in an addiction, in any case. In my experience meditation helps desensitize me to the emotional pain I am going through. The memories of what has happened through the day – or week or year – pop into my consciousness. I gently let them go. Another memory pops up. I gently let it go. I know these memories exist, I know these people exist, but I am teaching my brain not to be disturbed by them. The result is that I am able to relate to these people in a different way in real life. My brain has practiced not being disturbed by them. And when I see them again I have more resources to respond calmly.

Research is presently showing that when a stressful event happens all of us will respond with physical alertness. Depending how much stress there is in the interchange, I may feel a burst of adrenaline. My body is readying itself for fight or flight. A physical, neurological alert is a necessary part of life in the midst of relationships. What the research is showing is that people who use mindfulness practices are more able to return easily to a calm physical state. In other words, the natural response of the body and brain is to react in emotion, which readies us for action. If our brain does not know how to return to calm we stay alert and emotionally charged, tending to fight or to flee. But those who practice mindfulness have taught their brains to return to calm easily, so the interchange does not become charged with unnecessary energy. They are then more in control of themselves and therefore of the situation.

The energy of life comes from our emotions. Living fully does not mean living with repressed or hidden emotions. Rather, it is enjoying emotions but not being controlled by them. In one of my psychology classes two students presented a seminar about emotions. They played us an excerpt from *The Lion King* – music, colour, movement, fun. Then they turned down the sound – no music, and turned to black-and-white. 'This is what life is like with no emotion', they said. It was a simple illustration of the importance of emotion in our relationships. But relationships don't work if we don't know how to own our own feelings, or how to understand what our feelings are telling us. Owning our own feelings is recognizing that my feelings are inside my boundaries and are my responsibility.

❹ Across the Boundaries: Self-disclosure and Feedback

In the introduction I imagined life as a game of football – with blindfolds on. Relationships are complex and we are guessing about each other most of the time – and then speaking different languages when we try and talk about it. No wonder many of us revert to more simple topics – like quantum physics or neurophysiology!

The last chapter was an initial look at feelings and identifying them. When it comes to other people's feelings and reactions the complexities multiply. Yet if relationships are to work effectively we need to have some inkling of what life is like for the other person.

Walk a mile

A first step in learning to interpret or understand another person is to follow the old adage and walk a mile in their shoes. What would *I* feel like if I had just lost my job, had an argument with my girlfriend, heard that my son had been rejected from the course he was hoping for? Of course what *I* would feel like may be a very rough approximation of what the other person feels, but it's a start. I may need to add a few qualifiers – What would *I* feel like if I had just lost my job, and I had a family of three children, and a high rent and had overcommitted myself on paying for the car? And it was the job I'd always dreamed of.

While this sounds like a deceptively simple thing to do, many of us don't do it. It's a bit like learning people's names – the most important thing to do is listen when they're introduced. Or like learning the art of good conversation, by first learning to listen to what the other person says. The fact is that we are usually working out what *we* will say, or listening to see if *my* name is said correctly. The most basic thing of all in relationships is to discipline myself to listen to the other person and then, if I want to understand what life is like for them, to put myself in their shoes. Sometimes we don't do that because we simply don't want to. I don't want to know what it feels like to be a refugee desperate to be accepted into a safe country, risking my life to get there. I don't want to imagine how it feels to have a sick wife, or an alcoholic mother, or to be getting old and facing death. The most profound gift I can give another person is to gain some understanding of what their life is like, to care what their feelings are in the midst of pain.

When we watch a movie or read a novel we can be practicing this exercise to a greater or lesser degree. Those who cry over a romantic tragedy or come out of a political movie stirred up to do something about injustice are those who are walking a mile in someone else's shoes. Those of us who are less moved, more blasé, may need to practice this exercise more. A male friend of mine assures me that many men do not experience this. Their reaction may be 'Gee, that would be hard' – but they don't actually experience the emotion of the other person. They need to learn this in a whole new way.

Try it:

Think of a conversation, a movie, a book or a TV show you experienced in the last week. Name the reactions of the other people. What were they feeling?
What would it be like to feel what they did?
When have I felt like that?
What was it like?

Relationships work most effectively, most intimately, when we care enough about the other person to imagine what their life is like from the inside. This does not mean I have to carry their pain, or tell them how to solve the problems of their life. In fact the relationship works better if I don't do that; if I know what *their* pain is and what *mine* is – what is inside my boundaries and what is not – but I listen enough to be able to have some understanding of life looking out through their eyes.

This might sound like an awful lot of guesswork, and it is. The best way to know how someone else feels is still to ask them to tell you. Our guesses can go wrong. Our histories will lead to different perceptions. Asking, 'What's that like for you?' is one of the most powerful relationship builders there is.

A window into relationships

Two men, Joe and Harry, were puzzling how to express this neatly, how to draw a diagram that helps us understand how relationships can be deepened. They came up with a deceptively simple diagram and called it after themselves; the Johari window.[6]

	What you know	**What you don't know**
What I know	**Open** What we both know	**Secret** What I know but you don't
What I don't know	**My blind spots** What you know but I don't	**Unknown** What neither of us know

The window is made from looking at what I know (about me) and what I don't know; and from what you know about me, and what you don't know. In any given relationship there will be parts of myself that we both know about – this is the open window. There will be parts of myself that I know but which I don't let you see – the secret part. Parts of myself which you see but of which I am unaware are my blind spots. And there are parts that neither of us know – that are unknown to both of us.

At the beginning of a relationship the window that is open – that part of me that we both know – is relatively small, because you don't know me very well yet.

Open	Secret
Blind spots	Unknown

As time goes on, and we continue to relate and talk about ourselves, you get to know more of me, so the 'open' window gets bigger, and the 'secret' window becomes relatively smaller. The process of self-disclosure opens the open window further, and diminishes the secret one.

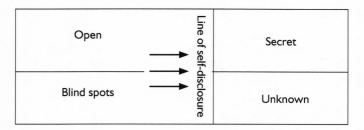

As we continue to get to know each other and our relationship becomes more honest you may also give me some feedback, telling me some things that you notice about me, of which I was unaware. This enables my blind spots to come to light – so the open window between us is enlarged again.

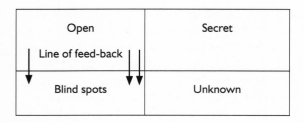

As I said, the diagram is deceptively simple. All we have to do is self disclose, and give feedback, and the window of relationship is open between us! Self disclosure and feedback are much more challenging than that simple sentence makes them sound.

Self-disclosure

Self-disclosure is not just talking. It is not sharing objective information, or telling stories I've told many times before. Rather, it's letting you see something of the real me. There are some people I have met with whom I immediately feel safe, as though I have known them for years. And I am thus quick to take down my guard and share something of my soul. There are other people I have known for years and it still feels as though we hardly know each other, as though somehow we only share information and not ourselves, as though we both have armour on up to our noses. What makes the difference? Past history of course, and who that person reminds me of, and who I remind them of, and the roles we have in each others' lives. But it is more than that. There is a mystery in how relationships work, how self-disclosure opens us.

I can give you information for years to come but not be opening myself to you. Or I can be a little more vulnerable and share my opinions or beliefs, attitudes or values. Or I can share past experiences. But if I really want intimacy, I will eventually share what it is like for me on the inside, what I am feeling.

Levels of intimacy:
Cliché
Information and facts
Opinions and beliefs
Feelings
Transparency e.g. needs

The most superficial level is to talk in clichés, which give no information at all. The next level is to share information and facts. These are outside of me and so do not necessarily let you see inside me at all. I can keep my mask in place and talk about the weather, the state of the nation, facts and figures.

Opinions and beliefs tell you more about me – how I see things, my perceptions, my preferences or my political or religious beliefs. When I was a child it was not really polite to talk about politics and religion. Those topics could cause disagreement, so they were off-limits. Today it is more acceptable – but still many people only talk about 'politically correct' versions of politics and religion.

The deeper level is to talk about feelings. This is really removing my mask and letting you into my inner world. This is a more difficult world to find the words for. And often we are left feeling vulnerable. This is the place of intimacy and accepting each other as we are. Deeper again is transparency, for example talking about my needs.

This process is not about quantity. Nor is it even about choosing to share at deeper levels. It is a quality of relationship, a willingness on my part to be vulnerable – to let you see the real me. I have learned to try and listen with the inner ear, to notice what is happening in my heart. It is difficult to find the words to even talk about this. It is something we each have to practice within ourselves. It is the opposite of just sharing information; it is an intentional lowering of my guard. I can imagine some people saying, 'But why would I want to do that?' And the answer is, 'Because that is what makes relationships effective.' Being vulnerable, letting you see me for who I am without my armour, without my mask. Some of us tend to do this too quickly, trust too readily. It is wisest to do it a little at a time, test the waters, check the response. I don't have to expose all my vulnerabilities to everyone for the sake of a few good relationships.

There is a big difference between how extroverts and introverts share themselves. Extroverts tend to talk instead of thinking; they are much more practiced at putting everything into words. Introverts, on the other hand, think instead of talking. They need an invitation to talk. They often don't understand that the extroverts are working out what they think by speaking. The introvert is so busy thinking what they plan to say that they might even forget to say it.

Extroverts are better at talking and interacting, although that does not necessarily mean that they are better at true self-disclosure. It often just means that extroverts are better at talking with their armour on. They have a more practiced mask. Self-disclosure is not about the quantity of words – it is about the quality of what I say, what I share, how much of myself I put into it. This is where the inner ear is important. I listen to myself from the inside. Try to honestly notice what is happening for me, whether I am sharing myself or keeping myself hidden.

Extroverts, then, may go deeper than information, may tell you their opinions and beliefs, and stories about themselves, and even their feelings, but you can tell their guard is still up. As the extrovert listens with the inner ear she learns to lower her guard rather than just entertaining, or filling the space with words.

I met a delightful extrovert on the first evening of a month-long intensive course. She happened to be the only extrovert at a table of introverts, so she entertained us with stories and jokes, filled in the awkward silences and made us feel welcomed. After a while she said, 'Look, I know I'm an extrovert and I need to give you introverts space so you can talk too. So I will be quiet for a while.' She sat in silence for perhaps five seconds, while the rest of us wondered what to say. Then she broke the silence, 'Okay you've had your chance, let me tell you another story.' She was joking, and we did all eventually take part in the conversation. But her act helped me understand a little more about introverts. Not only do we need a space of silence to start to share ourselves, but most of us also need an invitation; we need to know that the other person is really interested or we will not share our vulnerable inner world.

Try it

How easily do you self-disclose, and who with?

Extroverts tend to interact easily with strangers, whereas
introverts are more likely to self-disclose with one or two trusted
friends. Who do you prefer to interact with?
When you are in a conversation, are you most often focusing on
information, opinions or feelings?
How easy is it for you to take off your mask in a conversation?

For self-disclosure to be effective in developing relationships,
there needs to be two-way interest and vulnerability. To really get
to know someone else we both need to share our feelings – and
we both need to know that the other person is safe enough for
me to drop my guard a little and share myself with them. The
two-way relationship only works well if we learn to really listen to
the other person. And really listening can be surprisingly difficult.

The other side of self-disclosure – listening, questioning, reciprocating

As I said earlier, the best way to find out what someone is feeling
is to ask them. Surprisingly the supposed 'Counsellor's Question'
– 'How does that make you feel?' is not the best one to ask. It
tends to make me go to my head to analyse what I am feeling. The
more simple question, 'What's that like for you?' allows the other
person to stay with their inner experience and talk about it. And
the best way I can help them to talk is to listen without judgment.
We intuit judgment in each other surprisingly easily.

If our relationship is to be mutual – a relationship of equals
– we both need to share similarly. I need to be self-disclosing,
to be vulnerable enough to let the openness of the relationship
happen; and I need to respect and encourage your self-disclosure.
If there is not a reciprocity, a relatively equal sharing, then the
relationship is uneven – as is the case in counselling relationships,
or mentoring, or helping. This is not wrong – it is just a different
kind of relationship. A relationship between friends or lovers needs
to be fairly even to be effective and safe.

If one person always asks the questions, and the other tends to self-disclose, the relationship will get out of step. We both need to listen and we both need to talk. Extroverts will need to practice listening more, introverts need to talk, probably more than they are comfortable with, although it is surprising how much an introvert will talk once they know they really have an interested audience who values their inner world.

Listening

How we question and how we listen can make all the difference in the unfolding of a relationship. Listening well is really the foundation of good relationships. It takes practice but certainly can be learned. Being truly interested in the other person's world is the starting point. Wanting to know what life is like for them enables me to listen with interest when they speak. Of course, this interest needs to be genuine. We have all experienced a question from someone who is just helping to keep a conversation going by asking more. We have seen their eyes glaze over when they do not listen to the answer. As we cultivate true curiosity we ask genuine questions that encourage others to tell their story openly. Most of us need to know we are being listened to – a phrase, word or reflection can be enough to keep even an introvert talking.

Courses in counselling and interpersonal communication teach the basic skills, but they can easily be learned in everyday interactions. Often the hardest part is getting over the awkwardness of speaking in a way we are not used to, but practice soon makes the words come naturally.

The most straightforward way to show you are listening is to say a tiny part of what the person has just said, back to them. 'You felt really let-down.' 'You wondered what was going to happen next.' 'You had a fantastic time.' 'You thought she didn't understand you.' 'You felt like he saw right through you.' The point is to communicate (without saying it directly), 'I'm listening. I heard what you said.' Even a couple of words can be sufficient to give the message. 'Really let-down.' 'A fantastic time.' 'Right through you.' Staying with the person's own words, or very close to them, is safest.

If the person says a lot, or you lose track — maybe you were even distracted for a moment — you can stay with the last sentence they said. They usually stop to see if you've heard, to check if you still want them to go on. Saying a little of what you last heard communicates your interest.

Of course, if you are not interested it doesn't work too well! People are on the look-out for real concern. And our body language needs to communicate interest as well. One of the exercises I do is to get students to brainstorm how they behave when they don't want to listen. Even those who didn't realize they knew it can describe the body language of 'not-listening'. Looking away, fiddling, breaking eye-contact, turning away, staring unblinkingly, leaning backwards, folding your arms. Listening is the opposite — leaning slightly forwards, making eye-contact (and breaking it occasionally), sitting still with an open posture (facing towards the person with arms uncrossed). The words and the body language are only the surface of the communication, the 'technical' side of it. If you really are interested, that makes all the difference. The reflected phrases, the words that demonstrate your interest and hearing, are the skills which communicate your concern, your desire for the relationship to deepen.

Some of us need much more practice in this than others. Some people have learned to listen just by being part of conversations. Others have habits of not listening, of cutting across what the person is saying with a question, or starting on a new topic of conversation. Saying back to the person a little of what they have said is a discipline, but a very effective way to deepen a relationship. In my experience most people want someone to listen to their inner world. But they check out their listener carefully. If you begin to give advice, or problem solve, or tell your own story, they will shut the doors.

I call
this the
ski-slope
of learning
listening skills. We
all already have our
ways of listening – we
have been doing it for
years already. So when we
start doing it a different way,
it is like climbing up a ski-slope.
Once we practice, it gets easier and
easier, more and more natural and a
normal part of our way of conversing, and
it becomes a reflex.

Try it:

Over the next few days try one reflective statement in every conversation. Not a question, just a reflection of a little of what the person just said. Using the sentence starter – 'It sounds as though...' or 'You thought.../felt...' is a good way to begin. Notice the person's response. Usually it is 'Yes,' and then they continue the story. If you do it too often – especially if this is new for you – they might think you are acting strangely. You're still going up the ski-slope! If you know someone else who will practice it on you, all the better. You can then experience the process from the other side, and learn what works best for you to communicate: 'I'm interested, I'm listening.'

Questions

Questions are also important in showing I am interested and listening, but surprisingly are not as effective as the listening statements described above. That's because questions *usually* originate with the listener's agenda – not the speaker's. Television interviews demonstrate this almost unequivocally. The interviewer has his own agenda and asks questions to find out what he wants to know. A truly self-disclosing relationship does not work that way. Questions which carefully follow what the person has just said are therefore the most effective. 'What's that like for you?' (although initially a little unnatural), is one of the most effective because it so clearly links to the speaker's own experience.

Questions which are open-ended are much more user-friendly than closed questions. Closed questions are ones which require a one-word answer, usually yes or no. They can bring the conversation to an abrupt halt, especially if they are not close to what the person was trying to express. Open questions are questions which open the way for further explanation. 'You were saying he didn't seem to understand you, what was happening that made you think that?' 'How did you think the evening went?' 'What was the course you were planning on doing?' How, when, where, what and who questions can lead to further exploration.

Again, putting yourself in the other person's shoes can be the best way to generate the right questions to ask. Trying to put yourself in their world may help you realize how little you understand, and this in itself will provoke questions. Learning to be curious is one of the most effective ways to help us develop questions. A delightful, and rather unorthodox counsellor I know decided to have a cat tattooed on the inside of her wrist to remind her to be curious and explore the *other* person's world, rather than giving her own answers.

But too many questions can turn a conversation into an interview. It is best to return to reflective statements described above, after one or two questions. When someone asks too many questions I find myself becoming sensitive – I begin to feel as though they are trying to evaluate me or have somehow shifted to their own agenda. If, however, after a time, they tell me a little of their story which is relevant, the conversation becomes more 'even' again. Sharing something of our own story can be a way of empathizing.

Try it

Think of a conversation you have had in the last week. Try to remember what the other person was talking about.
How much do you know about what they were telling you?
What questions can you think of now that you could ask if the conversation came up again? What are some things you could be curious about?

Empathy

Empathy is 'feeling with' the other person, understanding a little of what life is like from the inside. It is not the same as sympathy, which is closer to feeling sorry for a person. Empathy is more equal, an understanding of having been in similar places.

I have been quite fascinated in the last few years to hear something of the research in 'mirror neurons.' Mirror neurons are the parts of our brain which recognize what is happening for the other person. To an extent they are the 'neurology' of empathy. MRI scans (Magnetic Resonance Imaging) are enabling neurologists to see what part of the brain is responding in a given situation. Researchers are able to see that when you are feeling, or doing, or even intending something, the same neurons in my brain will be activated, and it is as though I, too, experience what is happening for you. True empathy is not feeling your feelings, but it is sensing something of what it is like for you – and feeling for you. The research shows that the mirror neurons of people with autism are not functioning in this way. So a child with autism is unable to experience what it is like for the other person, and so cannot respond appropriately.

In some ways we are all a little 'autistic', caught in our own world and lacking empathy for others. The delightful book *The Curious Incident of the Dog in the Night-time* by Mark Haddon[7] gives some insight into autism, and reveals to all of us a little of our own relationship difficulties. Mark Haddon writes as though he is Christopher, a fifteen-year-old boy with autism, who must use all the clues he can to understand people's strange behaviour. He is intelligent and knows every capital city in the world and all the prime numbers up to 7057, but he doesn't experience empathy and cannot interpret 'from the inside' what is happening for other people, and so must work everything out intellectually. Christopher's social worker Siobhan tries to help him to understand people by showing him what different facial expressions mean. But it doesn't work. Christopher explains why: 'I got Siobhan to draw lots of these faces and then write down next to them exactly what they meant. I kept the piece of paper in my pocket and took it out when I didn't understand what someone was saying. But it was very difficult to decide which of the diagrams was most like the face they were making because people's faces move very quickly.' In contrast Christopher likes dogs because, 'You always know what a dog is thinking. It has four moods. Happy, sad, cross and concentrating. Also, dogs are faithful and they do not tell lies because they cannot talk.'

While true autism seems to be a neurological impairment, some people have similar difficulties simply because they have not learned how to empathize, have not practiced what it was like to put themselves in someone else's shoes.[8] We can learn to empathize by intentionally listening and asking the other person to tell us how the experience was for them.

The other part of learning empathy and how to show it is learned by feedback. Feedback is the other major way to open our windows of relationship.

Feedback

Feedback is the process whereby I tell my friend what our relationship is like from my side. Feedback is being able to say, 'When you shout I want to withdraw from you' or 'When you insist on paying it makes me feel you want to be in control.' Feedback is telling the other person what you see in them – looking from the other side of the relationship.

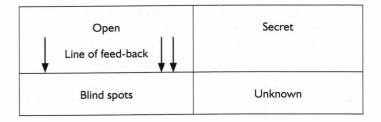

Most of us do not give feedback well, or even avoid giving it altogether. More often it is part of more formal relationships, or learning-teaching relationships – even then it is a sensitive area. Usually feedback needs to be given only in the context of permission. A training/mentoring relationship can contain feedback because the student is wanting to learn and so has, at least implicitly, given permission to the teacher to give him information on his performance. I want to know if I am changing gear properly, holding the racquet correctly, pitching my voice far enough, following the rules of academic referencing and so on. Within that context I have declared myself a learner, needing input from others. Most of us, in our day-to-day relationships, don't acknowledge ourselves as learners. If we did it would make feedback a lot easier.

Try it

Ask a friend to give you some feedback. Think specifically of an area where you are a novice and they are an expert. Tell them that you recognize their expertise in that area and ask for some feedback on your own performance in that area. For some of us this will still be a vulnerable place to start – but acknowledging the need to learn is a great way to get helpful input.

Be grateful for the feedback – it may not be given again.

This little exercise contains an important principle in giving and receiving feedback – the principle of control. Receiving feedback puts us in a vulnerable position, so holding on to the control is a way to keep it safe. If I ask for feedback I am in control and I can also halt the process. 'Thank you for the input, I will think about that' can close the interaction once I have had enough. While in a true training situation some of us will want all the feedback we can get, most of us are more sensitive around relationship issues. We have already been practicing our present style of relationship for a long time and we don't necessarily want to change. Our relational patterns feel like part of ourselves, and we don't want other people trying to change us — it feels too close to rejection.

If there is something we really want to say to someone, some feedback we want to give before we burst, we need to ask permission. Many of us don't say anything until something goes wrong and then we erupt, expressing ourselves badly. Asking permission is often awkward, but much more effective in the long run — and the very fact that it is awkward means that I too am somewhat vulnerable. 'Can I talk to you about what happened last week?' or 'Remember you said such and such to me, can I talk about that?' or, 'I've been thinking about how we've been getting on lately. Can we talk about that?'

Years ago I took part in training in pastoral counselling with a small group of others. At the end of the training we were invited to give our peers some feedback. Feedback from peers can be one of the most daunting kinds of comments. This may well be because we all accept that our teacher is more expert than we are, but a natural comparison and evaluation is present among peers.

Given this peer-learning context, we were instructed very specifically on how to give the feedback — and the actual words we had to say showed us that really our feedback was simply trying to change the other person to be more like ourselves. The words we had to say to prefix our feedback were 'Peter, you should be more like me and….' For over thirty years I have remembered what I said because it was such a powerful learning. 'Peter you should be more like me — and be less religious in the way you talk to people.' The point was that I found the religious talk uncomfortable. I wasn't really giving Peter feedback, I was saying what I wanted, I was trying to change him.

I am not suggesting that we should put these words, 'You should be more like me,' into our feedback – at least not out loud! I am suggesting that we check our own motives when giving feedback – usually we are trying to change the other person to make them more similar to us.

Specific and honest

Another important aspect of giving feedback is to be specific. 'You were fantastic!' or 'You did that so badly,' are not helpful feedback comments. 'When you interrupt me before I've finished my sentence I feel as though you are not listening,' is specific feedback. Pinpointing the exact thing a person does or says is the most useful way to give feedback. It also makes us think specifically about their behaviour and check whether we are just trying to make them clones of ourselves.

The second part of a feedback sentence can also be essential – the feedback about my own feelings. This is part of owning my own feelings and vital to making the relationship work. 'When you tell me how I ought to do things I feel put down, as though you think I am dumb.' 'When you yell at the kids I find myself cringing. It reminds me of my mother yelling at me.' 'When you tell me where we are going to go without checking if I want to, I feel devalued.' While this is not relevant in a teaching-type context, in an ordinary relationship it is crucial. It admits what is happening for me. It lets the other person know what effect their behaviour has on me – and it gives them the free choice of responding to my reactions or not. It stops the feedback being a cloning exercise and turns it into an open, honest, two-way relationship.

Another way to help make giving critical feed-back palatable is the 'sandwich' principle. Find something positive – and honest – to say, then give the feedback, then add something else positive. Sandwich the corrective part between two appreciations. 'I've noticed how much you are helping with the younger kids. When you yell at them though, I find myself cringing. It reminds me of my mother yelling at me. I really appreciate that you are wanting to keep them in line.' 'I really like it that we are spending so much time together. There is one thing though. When you tell me where we are going to go without checking if I want to, I feel devalued. Can we talk about that? I really appreciate that we are able to share things together.' 'I really liked the music you were playing last night. I'm wondering if it could be quieter after 10 o'clock. I was trying to get to sleep. Good choice of CD though.'

While these examples sound stilted, they are illustrating the pattern. In real life we have to find ways to relate what fits with our own style of communicating. Practicing while keeping the principle in mind is the key. Even giving positive feedback is outside the comfort zone of a lot of people. Starting with small amounts of positive feedback can get us over the hump to a more free way of give and take.

Try it

Think of someone you could give some positive feedback to, or someone who you have really been needing to talk to about something bothering you. Or if you haven't got a real situation, ask a friend if you can practice on them anyway! Role-playing, while rather unnatural, can be one of the best ways to learn. Think about the specifics of the feedback. What is it that you want to say? Be specific. What is your feeling about this situation? Can you put that into words also? If what you are going to say is negative, think of positives you can say as well. If it helps, tell the person you are practicing communication patterns and ask for their feedback on how you did it!

This chapter has largely focused on the 'technical skills' of communicating across the boundaries. These skills can make all the difference in communicating, hearing the other person and letting them know we are hearing them. The skills, while powerful, are not sufficient in themselves – our real *experience* of a person is the true core of the relationship. This is the subject of the next chapter.

❺
Real Relationships – or Roles

Role-specifying relationships
In the last chapter I mentioned training or mentoring relationships. Obviously different relationships work in different ways. The main focus of this book is relationships between equals. Of course there are many principles about relationships which apply across the board – respect, trust, boundary-keeping and so on. However, in general, roles change the way a relationship works. With a role comes certain expectations and preconceived ideas. The main aim of this book is to explore the principles which make relationships most effective, which can then be applied to a greater or lesser degree depending on the effect of role and context. If I am in a position relating to someone who is superior to me in an organization, already – almost always – my ability to relate openly and honestly is limited. Suffice to say this book is talking about the ideal conditions – relationships between equals.

Organizational charts tend to define roles in terms of rank, or position, with line authority showing who is superior and who must report to whom. This immediately changes the way people relate to each other. In some ways it makes relationships safer – expectations are defined and people just 'get on with the job' demanded of them. Their purpose is not to 'have a good relationship' but to 'get the job done', so it is accepted that relationships do not work the same way as they would in a different environment.

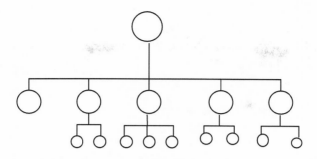

An organizational chart that shows rank and authority

While organizations assign roles, many people also assign roles in their heads. They evaluate their relationships in terms of older–younger, expert–novice, superior–inferior, experienced–inexperienced, family–outsider, religious–nonreligious. In other words, they are using internal criteria to place themselves over or under the other person. This strategy may help them decide how to act with other people in a predetermined way, but it is not conducive to an open relationship between equals. More mature relationships do not work by prescription of role. They work through the principles of respect, boundaries, self-disclosure and feedback.

Another way people categorize others is by using the pair of concepts same–different. It is as though they have an internal radar deciding who is the 'same' and who is 'different' – and therefore who is 'in' and who is 'out', who is to be trusted and who is not. They don't tend to tell people what their criteria are, but their radar is working in order to keep themselves safe. In times of stress and danger we are all tempted to use our radar systems, and to close ranks with those who are the 'same' as we are. Again, mature relationship-building is about extending bridges across difference, accepting people who are 'other' than ourselves, learning from them, being open to them. It needs to be acknowledged that we have internal ways of evaluating other people because we role-cast each other and this will hinder the free flow of equal relationship.

The tendency to categorize, to rank and to organize is part of the way we make sense of the world – but it tends to work against deeper relationship building. One of the most important ways to consistently develop deeper relationships is to declare power differences and to be open about role expectations.

Another kind of role taking

Roles can be designated for us, or we can act 'in-role' in the way we relate by designating role inside our heads. Eric Berne called this kind of role-taking *The Games People Play*,[9] suggesting that we 'play the game' of being a child, adult or parent in our relationships. Each person takes a role in response to the other and Berne called the subsequent interpretation of the interaction of those roles transactional analysis. If two people acted and reacted as reasonable, responsible adults, the interaction was named adult–adult. If one person behaved like an irresponsible child, and the other person reacted like a parent in response – admonishing or nurturing the 'child' – this was seen as a parent–child interaction.

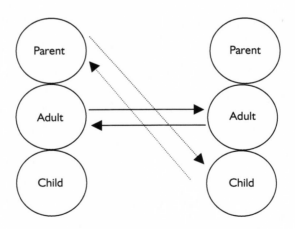

Two kinds of relationship interaction

As long as the two people interacting 'play the same game', the relationship continues to function fairly smoothly. While it may not be particularly healthy for one adult in a relationship to continually 'act like a child,' the relationship will function as long as the two people are in *agreement* about their roles. If the lines in the diagram above are parallel, then the two people are playing the same game – two adults can be reasonable together, two 'children' can play together, a parent and a child can stay with their chosen roles. When, however the two people 'play different games' the relationship becomes tricky.

If one person tries to act in an adult–adult way – being reasonable and responsible and discussing options, for example – and the other insists on childishly expecting to take no responsibility, appealing to the other person to act like a parent towards them, the relationship is in trouble. What has happened is that one person has taken on a hidden role – and tried to manipulate the other person to take on the complementary role.

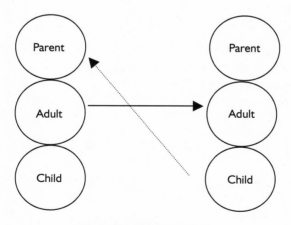

Playing different games

As children grow into adults, some parents have difficulty in allowing them to step out of the child role. The parent continues to act in the parent–child relationship, while the grown-up child may be trying to relate adult to adult. The relationship becomes difficult as the two sets of interactions collide.

Understanding the interaction by analyzing these processes is called transactional analysis because it gives a way to interpret the 'transactions' or interactions. It is reasonably easy much of the time to look at someone's behaviour and see whether they are acting as a responsible (or critical) parent, a reasonable adult or a playful, irresponsible child. Berne was not saying it was right or wrong to take these positions, rather, he was giving a way to analyze whether the relationship was working or not.

Try it

Think of a relationship which functions smoothly, and which you are happy with. Try to identify the role – in terms of parent, adult or child – that each of you is taking. Is it an adult to adult role? If not, are the lines of transaction parallel – for example, parent to child and child to parent – or are you both taking a child role?
Now think of a relationship which does not function smoothly. Can you identify which role – parent, adult, child – each person is taking? Again notice whether the lines are parallel – or whether they are crossed, that is, one person trying to relate in an adult to adult fashion, while the other insists on taking either a child or parent role.
Is it possible to talk with the person concerned?

The shift from child to adult

Over the last few years there has been a sharpening focus on the difficulty for men in defining when and how they become men. For a girl the onset of menstruation is a clear demarcation of her body's ability to mother a child, and therefore to be 'adult' and responsible. For a boy the line is much less clear.

In numbers of cultures an initiation experience clarifies the line of adulthood for the boy. Indigenous societies have various rituals in which a boy learns how to be a man. Jews celebrate the bar mitvah with the thirteen-year-old adolescent. But generally in Western society there is no such adult-initiated ritual to constructively welcome the boy into adulthood. Young men sometimes create their own experiences – often around driving cars, alcohol or sexual experiences. It has been suggested that initiation ceremonies could greatly help young men in their search for identity and self-acceptance.[10]

These practices help young men make the transition from acting out of the irresponsible 'child' role to taking on a more adult interaction pattern. As long as society ignores the adolescent need to define oneself as an adult in a constructive way, men will struggle to make the shift into adulthood.

Try it

If you are male try to identify what markers there were for you, to indicate your transition to being adult.

Were there ways adults (men in particular) welcomed you into adulthood?

Were there ways you and your peers attempted to make rituals or experiences to mark the transition?

What is your sense now of being an adult rather than a boy or an adolescent?

If you are female, think about your own onset of menstruation and recall your feeling around this indication of womanhood and fertility.

What was that experience like for you?

Was it shameful, or an occasion for celebration?

Did you feel welcomed into adulthood?

Reflect on this experience in comparison with brothers or boys you knew and their experience of puberty.

Another way – a less travelled road

M. Scott Peck, the psychiatrist who wrote the best-seller, *The Road Less Travelled*,[11] became a facilitator for companies and communities who wanted to develop relationships, who wanted to experience real 'community' in their organizations. In *A World Waiting to be Born: Civility Rediscovered*[12] he identifies the stages along the way to deeper relationships in a community context. His stages give important understanding for how relationships develop.

The first stage is that of pseudo-community. This is the time in any relationship before we know each other. Most of us are polite to people we don't know. So the beginning of a relationship is polite and pleasant. We are nice to each other, but we do not *know* each other. Many of our relationships will stay in pseudo-community for the whole lifetime of the relationship, because we do not need to know that person any further than the surface. I am polite to the assistant in the corner shop, I am polite to my dentist, and to all students making enquiries about courses, to the coffee-shop waitresses and to the manager of my townhouse complex. I am pleasant and courteous to all these people, but I do not know them and they do not know me.

Our society socializes us to be polite to each other – it makes for more smoothly running interactions. Travelling overseas alerts us to cultural differences – and different kinds of politeness. In Japan the first customer of the day is bowed to by all the shop assistants. I'm sure I appeared rude to many Japanese as I had not been socialized into bowing in return. In other countries people's lack of response seemed rude to me – but they understood each other perfectly. I'm sure Australia's off-hand casualness appears rude to other nationalities at times and as a result we offend overseas visitors. My point is that each society has its rules of politeness which helps the people of that society interact smoothly. The patterns are essential for everyday interactions – but they are not deep relationship and cannot be substituted for deep relationship.

Sooner or later, if we continue in relationship with someone, we will discover things about them that we do not like, that we disagree with, that we would like to change. The honeymoon is over and I have begun to see below the surface. If all my relationships are 'nice' it is likely I am not being honest about my reactions, or I am afraid to jeopardize seemingly-safe relationships. The fact is, there is something in everyone that I won't like if I am honest, and there are parts of me that people won't like as well. This is part of being human, and growing up means learning how to accept difference.

Chaos as positive

This stage of relationship building M. Scott Peck calls chaos, because differences emerge and the superficial sameness of pseudo-community is disrupted. Peck says that the natural response to difference is to try to heal, fix and convert. I see the difference in you and I try to fix you. I realize you believe differently from me and I try to convert you. I see some of your wounds and I try to heal you. The problem with fixing, healing and converting is that it is *my* agenda. I feel happier when people are the same as me so I try to change them. It is the same motive as when I give feedback to people to try and make them clones of myself. I am really saying, 'You should be more like me.' When everybody is trying to fix, heal and convert each other, the result is chaos.

Many of us are very uncomfortable with chaos so we do one – or both – of two things. Many times we retreat to pseudo-community. I have tried to convert you and you have resisted so I retreat to polite distance. You have tried to fix me and I don't want to be fixed so I keep you at arm's length and smile through gritted teeth. Many clubs and churches and even families remain in perpetual pseudo-community, not venturing further because they so dislike being fixed, healed and converted – or they see chaos as uncivilized impoliteness and will not venture there.

The other way to escape chaos is through organization. When we cannot retreat from relationships but must work together most of us choose organization. We appoint roles and tasks. We appoint a chair and use committee rules. We draw up organisational charts and decide who will direct whom. We give some people power over others and we assign status and rank, and reinforce it with pay-differentials. It brings order out of the chaos but it does not bring true relationship. The escape-chaos-through-organization route tends to follow the well known organizational stages of forming, norming and performing. People believe that performing – producing the goods – will come out of a process of organization or 'norming' – accepting the dominant way of doing things, rather than accepting difference. Indeed this may be the shortest route to results, but it is not community, not real relationship.

In one-to-one relationships or small groups this escaping into 'organization' happens when we evaluate each other as lesser or better, older, wiser, superior, more expert – and so assign a role – an inferior–superior way of relating rather than a relationship of equals. Or we accept a role assigned to us – wives are to submit to their husbands, children should defer to their elders, people with a higher-status job, or more education, should be more directive, we should defer to the 'boss'. While these roles may bring some order to a relationship, they do not lead to depth and openness.

How, then, is a relationship to get ahead of the impasse of chaos – of wanting to fix, heal and convert? The fact is, many relationships don't. They go on for years with each person trying to make the other conform to what they want. We see it in families sometimes – every Christmas the usual round of arguments about how the others should be behaving. Then a backing off before the next round of converting and healing. Or some kind of accord agreed to by accepting one family member as the boss for a time. At least this seems better than constant bickering.

Marriages, of course, do it too – the implicit appointment of one partner as boss – as a way through the disagreements. Or a retreating to the corners of the ring, agreeing not to talk about certain things to keep the peace. You can sometimes see this in restaurants – the couples who are not talking are the ones who are using this method – they have learned to get along by keeping to fewer and fewer safe topics.

Emptiness

The only way through the impasse is to let go trying to change the other person. Scott Peck calls it emptiness – and he admits that some people will do anything rather than go there. Emptiness is coming to the point of saying that I do not have the answers for the other person, and I have no right to convert or fix them. Sometimes a relationship may stay in chaos for years because one or other of the partners cannot bring themselves to the place of letting the other person be who they are. There is something very challenging about accepting that I do not have the answers for other people. Emptiness necessitates accepting the other person as they are – warts and all. It is a choosing to value the good in the other person, and to accept the not-so-good as part of the package. It is a realization that humans are imperfect, and this is the way life is. Many of us do not want to accept this and so we fight it, for years perhaps.

Stages of a relationship

Pseudo-community	
Chaos	➤ Escape into organization
Emptiness	
Community – real relationship	

Emptiness sounds too much like dying – and sometimes feels like it. The thought of it makes many people retreat all the way back to pseudo-community, to politeness and distance, rather than stay with someone in their unhealed state. Years ago, when my marriage broke up, most of my friends stood with me, staying with me in the pain of failure and loss. But others would not accept my decisions and tried to convert me to their way of seeing things. Or to work out where I had gone wrong so they could fix me. To tell me which books I needed to read to make it all better. There is nothing like death and divorce to expose people's philosophy of life – the philosophy they think everyone should have.

I understand people wanting to fix my marriage. I have reacted the same way to others. Their marriage break-up feels as though it

threatens mine. Their giving up and walking away feels like letting
the side down. So I try to make them stay. The world is a safer
place if people have the same values as I do. Or so it seems.

Emptiness to community

The way of emptiness in a relationship is the only way through to
depth. Letting go is the birthplace of real life. Spring only follows
winter. Intimacy is the fruit of self-emptying. For some people this
will sound impossible. Or too scary to contemplate. I suggest an
exercise to help.

Try it

Think of your most intimate relationships, or intimate relationships
that you have seen. Try to identify the characteristics of these
relationships. Which of the stages do they seem closest to?
Pseudo-community, chaos, emptiness – or the community that
comes after emptiness?

What are the differences in your own relationships where you fix,
heal and convert – compared with those relationships where you
accept the other person without trying to change them?

The fruit of embracing emptiness is that we experience real
relationship, intimacy where I am known for who I am. And I
know the other person without trying to change them. It is a
rare experience for most of us and is only experienced in a few
relationships. It is being transparent and yet accepted for who I am.
No wonder we fight the process. Most of us are not comfortable
with transparency. Our masks are much safer.

The key process here is acceptance: a willingness to accept myself
as less than perfect; a willingness to accept the other as less than
perfect. While this is what we mean when we talk about tolerance
at its best, it is not the politically correct kind of tolerance. Political
correctness is pseudo-community – it makes for smoother sailing,
yes, but it is only skin deep. Politically correct tolerance tends to

be a lowest-common-denominator – a conformity to greyness. Real depth of acceptance brings a diversity of colour. On the one hand, political correctness may say I cannot sing Christmas carols, or wear the burka, or any other sign of difference, because it might offend your religion. On the other hand, political correctness says you can do anything – even hurtful practices such as female circumcision – because I mustn't disagree with what you think is your right. True relationship applauds difference, enjoying the richness it brings, and gives the other person freedom to be who they most truly are, while being honest about who I am. Relating only through roles and organization tends to define what a person can be, how they can act, what is most effective. Real relationships are much more untidy – but much more life-giving.

6
Distance to Intimacy

The last chapter explored the stages of 'community-making', the stages that groups tend to go through in their journey to being a community. Relationships follow similar stages, but are also complicated by the *kind* of relationship it is. Some relationships will always stay in the initial, being-polite-to-each-other stage, because we only relate over buying the milk, or paying for the petrol, or because our children play the same sport for a time. Others will be about basic companionship, doing things together, getting things done – and we do not expect closeness and intimacy.

Circles of closeness
Our relationships are like concentric circles around us – some distant, some close – some moving through the layers.

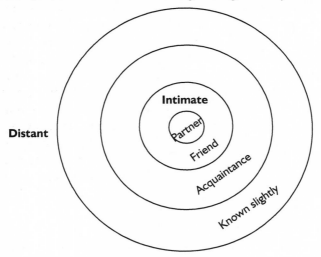

The outermost circle represents those people we see occasionally, who we may greet on the street, but really hardly know below the surface. They may be people we have known for years, may even potentially be good friends – or enemies – but we do not, at this point, know them. The next circle are acquaintances, people who we would chat to now and then and share some opinions or comments – usually on safe topics. It may be old classmates, people we have known more closely but now do not keep in touch. Or people we are beginning to know, perhaps in a work context where we share a little more than just exchanges about the weather. This circle may even include family members, who once we knew well, but have moved away from, either geographically or psychologically, and of whom we might say now, 'Really, they don't know me any more.'

Further in would be friends, or neighbours, or those that are in a group of mutual interest, or family members. We share our ideas and opinions, some beliefs maybe and a little of our feelings. Our relationship may have weathered some storms of disagreements, or pain and loss. These are the people I trust and would call on if I needed help.

The inner circle usually only contains one or two or a few very close friends or family members, my partner. This is someone with whom I share my soul, my innermost thoughts, my honest feelings. This is someone I can be open with when I am hurt by them, or angry with something they did. Some of us have no-one in this inner circle, or maybe only one or two in the space of our whole lives. Those of us who want to bring up children usually opt for a long-term intimate relationship if we can. If we are going to provide a secure environment for our children to grow up, we are most effective if we can learn how to relate intimately and honestly with our partner. This commitment to honesty and intimacy draws the relationship into the innermost circle.

Distance and quality

The Johari window can represent the differences in the relationships between those in the outer circle and those in inner circles. A relationship in the outer circle is characterized by only a small window of knowledge. You don't know a lot about me, and I don't know a lot about you or how you perceive me.

Relationships in the inner circle, in contrast, have a much bigger open window of relationship. You know a lot about me, I have self-disclosed a lot to you, and we are able to give and take feedback. We both know how the other sees us, and are willing to trust each other, taking down our defences.

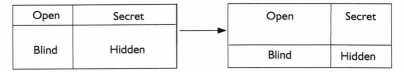

While the Johari window gives some insight into how relationships at the different levels operate, there are other differences, depending on the relationships themselves. Obviously there may be many layers of circles, and subtle differences between relationships. The main idea is simply that relationships are at different distances, and different levels of intimacy. Usually there is a mutuality about a relationship – if you are in my circle of friends, I am in your circle of friends. If there is a discrepancy, for example, you view me as an acquaintance, but I view you as a close friend, there will be different expectations and some disappointments in the relationship.

When we first came to live in Brisbane and began to make friends I would realize that this was happening. I would think of new friends as being in my inner circle of friendship because I had only a few relationships. They, of course, had years of friendships and people who were closer to them than I was. This kind of misunderstanding happens constantly in relationships as we have different expectations, family patterns, cultural differences. And of course there are personality differences, different needs and past learning, which has taught some of us to keep up our guard for years.

Try it

Think of a few people who are in the outer circle for you – people
who you know slightly – possibly by name, but maybe not.
Now name some acquaintances – in the next circle. How much
do you know about them?
Now name some friends. What makes the difference for you
between acquaintances and friends?
Who is in your innermost circle? What are those relationship/s
like for you?

Moving through the circles

Many of our relationships will stay in the same layer – a distance
that is comfortable for both of us. We tend to make some kind
of evaluation of the other person and decide at what distance
the relationship will operate. When we first meet someone that
relationship is necessarily in the outer layer, although some prior
knowledge of the other person may facilitate moving into a closer
level quickly. Usually there is a time lapse between moving from
one level to another. Mutual trust needs to be built, with a slow
gathering of knowledge about the other and shared exchanges.

Sometimes people try and move too quickly through the layers,
usually to their detriment. Romantic relationships are a prime
example. I'm sure I have fallen in love at first sight, and the other
person will be my friend and lover forever. I quickly self-disclose,
and expect the other person to do likewise. The gradual building
of trust does not occur, there is gradual recognition of similarities
and differences, and so my expectations and hope of true love
are disappointed. Occasionally love at first sight happens, fuelling
our hopes that such magic is possible. But usually relationships
grow step by slow step through sharing, disagreeing, listening,
conflicting and opening again; moving through the layers one
at a time, resting on the way and moving closer. A slow dance
of mutual self-disclosure and feedback. Too rapid a movement

through the layers is like the quick nakedness of a one-night-stand – self-disclosure and then a quick return to anonymity – not the stuff of real relationship.

Dan and Steve went to the same high school but didn't really know each other. They were in different classes and circles of friends, only meeting on common ground in the debating society. Steve travelled for a couple of years before starting university and Dan tried some different courses before settling to law. Then they found themselves both employed by the same law firm. They were polite and friendly in their responses to each other, gradually talking more as they met up at parties or the pub after work on a Friday afternoon. When Dan overheard Steve talking about a refugee camp he had visited while he was travelling he realized they had more in common than he had realized. He had been investigating ways he might put his training to use in legal requirements for refugees and immigrants. Dan invited Steve for a drink the following Friday and asked him more about his experiences. It wasn't long before they realized that while they had similar interests their approaches were very different. Steve's religious upbringing made him interested in helping people within that context whereas Dan was more concerned with policy and international legal relations. Dan found himself cautious about Steve's religious contacts and enthusiasm but was drawn by his obvious concern for people and his experiences.

Through school Dan and Steve were in the 'known slightly' layer. At work they are acquaintances. It is now a question of whether there is enough common ground for them to become friends, or whether their differences will keep them more distant. Usually, when we meet someone new, we are checking for common ground. We find the appropriate distance for the relationship depending on the similarities and differences between us. Generally we are attracted to people where there is a lot of similarity of attitudes, beliefs, interests, background – and enough difference to be stimulating. Dan and Steve are checking out their differences and exploring their common ground.

The building of relationships tends to move through stages. Stages of give and take, moving together, moving away, trusting, pulling back and trusting again. The first layer is like Peck's first level of community-building – the 'being nice' stage, pseudo-community. It is the level of being civilized. Our parents and education taught us to 'be nice' to each other, to be civilized little boys and girls. Most of us, thankfully, have carried that into adulthood. So I can expect the man at the petrol station to be polite to me, the woman at the checkout to smile and be courteous. I can assume that my colleagues will be civil when I appear at work, and that my students will show respect in my classes, to me and to each other.

Being civilized

Being civilized is an expected part of our society, and a necessary part of how a democracy works. There is a basic expectation of mutual respect and courtesy which enables everyday relationships to function smoothly. Most of our relationships will be civilized as a foundation for any further approach, and a lack of civility will warn us to keep our distance. However, being civilized is not the same as being honest. Civility can be an outer layer, like the oil that keeps machinery moving – a necessary part of life and society, but not to be mistaken for true depth. It is possible to smile over gritted teeth, to make a show of politeness for the sake of continued interaction. A necessary part of many aspects of social life, but not the place to live, not what one would hope for in one's family and friendships. Being civilized may hold within it the possibility of conflict, certainly the reality of undisclosed difference. Being civilized can be represented by a relationship that moves towards the other – but away, or against at the same time. That is, we know how to behave in a way that keeps the relationship functioning, but underneath we still have our guard up, we are smiling through our masks.

The representation of this stage is an arrow with a wide base. The arrow depicts a movement towards. The arrowhead is the civilized front – the positive image, the moving closer to you. The broad base is my defences. Behind my movement closer to you,

I am still holding up my shield. I do not know you yet and my guard is still up. I'm prepared to give you a chance, I'll be polite and courteous, but I will not disclose too much too quickly.

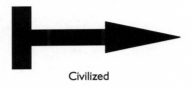

Civilized

An exception to this rule is opening my heart to a stranger on a bus, or an aeroplane, someone I have never met before. I may disclose far more than I would even to a friend. The reality is though that I have a different kind of shield up, a different kind of defence – I'm never going to see you again, my secrets are safe. Of course if you follow me home, decide you are going to move in, I might be sorry I had shared so much so quickly, and will have to find another way to distance myself! In fact people do this – distance themselves – in all sorts of ways. They move away geographically, pull down the shutters and don't make eye contact, stop inviting you to drinks or refuse to respond to your invitations. If we have moved too close too fast, we find ways to draw back, to signal that the relationship needs to be more distant. Most of us are not adept at saying so in words and so we do it in other ways, hoping that the other person gets the message.

The first level of a relationship, then, is rather ambivalent – sending messages of politeness, but also holding the other at arm's length. A distance is maintained in the relationship to allow time to check the other out, to find out if there are enough areas of similarity to enable the relationship to work at a closer span. To have a relationship with someone there needs to be some similarity, enough overlap, to facilitate communication, understanding and liking.

Common ground
Relationships are a mix of the two opposite proverbs, 'Birds of

a feather flock together' and 'Opposites attract.' We need some similarity to feel safe, to feel affirmed – but enough difference to add spice to the relationship, to add interest to the dynamic between us. Usually we move in to closer relationships when there is a lot of common ground. Depending on the personalities and histories of the two people, it seems that the closest relationship will discover enough similarity to experience a shared reality, but enough difference to be stimulating.

Little similarity   More overlap – but some difference

It is likely that the people in our inner circles are more like the overlap in the right-hand diagram than the left. In more distant relationships, being civilized allows us to handle the differences between us, to allow difference but keep it from being too threatening.

When we begin to move closer to someone else, it seems the natural impulse is to want the other to be more like me. If they are not like me, I tend to try to change them to make them more like what I am. This is the fixing, healing and converting that is an – often unacknowledged – part of many of our relationships. This is the process that our pastoral counselling trainers were trying to help us to see. If, when I comment on your behaviour, I must add in the phrase, 'You should be more like me,' I acknowledge the real underlying agenda in what I am saying.

Finding similarity and difference

Unexpectedly, the act of moving closer to someone else seems to contain implicitly a desire to change the other, to make them more like me. We seem to be seeking overlap, a mutuality in the relationship – and if it is lacking we try to construct it by moulding the other person, shaping some part of them to fit with what I want. For relationships to function well on a closer level, there needs to be some give and take, some reciprocity of influence. But if all the influence is one way, or if the influence is really coercion, there is unhealthiness in the relationship. When we first meet someone we are attracted to, especially in romantic relationships, there tends to be a lot of leeway of influence – I want you to like me so I'll become what you want. I want to like you so I will nudge you to change – and you respond and reciprocate – and at first there may be some delicious fireworks. It *seems* that we see things the same way, it *seems* we like doing the same things, it appears that we have met our 'soulmate', the mythical being who is the mirror image of myself.

But usually reason reasserts itself, we take off our rose-coloured glasses, we stop letting the other person mould us into their image and we see the, maybe all too obvious, differences. This may be the beginning of true relationship of accepting the other, but it does not feel like it and we often retreat – either to being civilized, or to trying to change the other again.

This dynamic process is the way in which we find at what distance each relationship works most beneficially. It is often painful. And some of us cling inappropriately to trying to keep relationships closer than is healthy; while others back off too soon, or too far, in order to keep from getting hurt. While I have described this process in terms of a romantic relationship, it occurs in all relationships, though probably less dramatically, and usually fairly subtly. Steve and Dan are in this process as they check the common ground between them. If Steve tries to convert Dan, literally, Dan is likely to back off – unless he sees something very attractive in what Dan is offering. If Dan tries to make Steve change his interest from helping refugees to international politics – along the line of his preferred political party – Steve is likely to back off.

The process of coming closer together almost always seems to contain the elements of influence – of fixing and converting. I want to influence your opinions, I want you to have better information, I want you to see the world as I see it. Or I want you to be more whole, to be less sensitive or less outspoken. Or I want your relationship with your children to be closer, or your skills to improve. The fact is that most of us want the world to be a better place, and we do it, relentlessly, by attempting to change people one at a time, to how we want our world to be. And most of the time we don't acknowledge that we are doing it.

The person who is loudly opinionated is trying to make everyone agree. The person who dominates conversations is trying to get others to see things from their viewpoint, or at least to give the semblance of it. And those of us who are more introverted, more withdrawn, do so in the hope that others will pull back a little also, become more sensitive. Or we are distancing ourselves in order to put energy into the relationships where influence is possible.

It may sound sceptical to perceive all relationships in this stage as an attempt to change the other person, but it is in recognizing this dynamic that we are most likely to relate in a more healthy, more reciprocal way. If I can recognize that I am dominating a conversation, because I am fearful of disagreement, I am more likely to be able to slow down, to hold my tongue and listen to your opinions. If I can acknowledge where I am trying to change you, I am more likely to forestall your distancing yourself to the safety of a merely civilized relationship. If the relationship is able to be respectful enough that I acknowledge my desire to influence you, and I give you the space to decide whether you want to be influenced or not, we are more likely to be able to move closer.

Being adversarial

To highlight the underlying tendency of this stage to be about healing, fixing and converting I have called this stage adversarial, even though most of the time we keep our civilized smile in place while we are doing it.

It is adversarial because we are, in essence, in opposition to the other person. We want them to be more like us and will try to make them so – often with the best of intentions – or so it seems.

'I am only trying to help', we say. But too often I am really trying to make my world safer.

I have represented this stage of the relationship as an arrow without the head to emphasize that the energy is about changing you – and therefore has an element of 'againstness' in it.

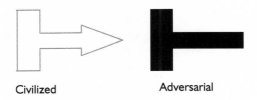

Civilized   Adversarial

It is very challenging during this period to concede that my way of seeing things is not the Right One, or the best, or the most informed. Usually relationships go back and forth between the civilized, being nice, and the adversarial, trying to change each other as we find the appropriate distance, or, eventually, find our way through to the next level. Families are especially frequently caught in the Adversarial stage. Families where the children are still at home experience the constant sandpaper of relationships. Extended families of grown-up children are bound by the family context – and geographical proximity – or repeated get-togethers at Christmas or birthdays. The family keeps us in relationship whether we like it or not, but we want the other to be different. Many family members would not be natural friends, would back off from a close relationship, but the family context keeps them in relationship, so the desire to change the other is continually stimulated.

Work colleagues similarly are held together by their work context but may not be natural allies. The drive to change the other or to distance oneself is constantly present in the work environment. Sometimes work colleagues divide into in-groups to allow those who are similar to support each other, and buffer the effects of the fixing and converting of other workmates.

The patterns of the adversarial process will often match the default positions of boundary styles. Those who are controllers – whether directly or by manipulation, will tend to try and push others to change. Those who are compliants will tend to step back from a crossed boundary, hoping the other will just somehow know their preference. If the boundary violation continues, they will step away into a more distant relationship. Or they will drop hints hoping the other will notice. The non-respondents will tend to stay in distant relationships, not hearing the requests of others to come closer. Avoidants will try and keep all relationships civilized, not wanting to make any trouble, maybe missing the 'Yes' of other people to draw closer.

We tend to play out our set patterns of relating in our family and work relationships. Friendships, on the other hand, can challenge us to different patterns, because we allow ourselves to be vulnerable enough to respond in different ways. Friendships are special relationships because they are relationships-of-choice. We distance ourselves from people we do not like, or who are not like us, but we choose to stay in a relationship with those with whom we have something in common. Held in a relationship by work, family, neighbourhood, we try to change each other, or find a way to keep our distance, moving between civility and adversariality.

Different institutions will use different methods to contain this dance. Parliamentary process is often openly adversarial, as the processes of change and power clash together. Churches, on the other hand, try to stay civilized, as being 'nice' is part of the expectation. Conformity tends to be the guiding principle, and change has to be done more subtly. Schools, hospitals and other institutions tend to have a rigid hierarchy, with roles, expectations and power clearly spelled out to make the direction of influence clear, and to keep civility as the public front.

All of this would seem to imply that we are forever caught in a conflict of trying to change each other or distancing ourselves. But there is a way through to intimacy. The fact that it is such hard work means that only a few of our relationships make it through to real closeness. Our friendships and committed relationships are the ones where we are most likely to experiment with different ways of relating, so we can move past the adversarial and civilized patterns.

Developing acceptance

Moving on from the adversarial stage necessitates lowering our defences, accepting that the other person is not like me, and that the person and the relationship is important enough to me that I will accept difference without backing off. This necessitates the surprisingly difficult task of letting go, of accepting the other person as they are without trying to change them. While this might be possible at a superficial level in the civilized stage, it is much more difficult in closer relationships. It is much easier to accept differences in people who are at arm's length; it is exponentially more difficult when they are in a constant relationship with me. We have to agree to differ, we have to accept the effects the differences bring about inside our own space.

This is the stage of true acceptance: non-conditional acceptance. It is not real acceptance if there are conditions attached, if I am still hoping to fix, heal and convert. It is letting go of my preferences, but still acknowledging my preferences. It is not the letting go of stepping back and being at a distance. It is letting go the conditions, the need to change you, while holding on to the relationship, holding on to the reality of who you are.

The tendency of the controller at this point in the relationship is still to try to change the other. The tendency of the compliant is to try to change themselves, or not to admit what they themselves actually want or prefer. Many Compliants, in what they would consider intimate relationships, are not able to identify what it is they desire themselves, because they are so occupied with giving the other what they want, or becoming what the other person wants. This course of action tends to have a 'use-by date'. Eventually keeping things under the surface doesn't work any more. Mid-life seems to galvanize us into a different way of being. Vietnam veterans who have held themselves together for twenty-five years seem to have to face their demons in their forties or fifties. Men who have hidden, even from themselves, a homosexual orientation, seem to have to acknowledge it at mid-life. Those of us in difficult marriages, or inappropriate work, seem to be able to manage for a quarter of a century but then some deep change surfaces and we see life differently. If we have a pattern of compliance we may well have hidden these difficulties, even from ourselves. But mid-life effects a change. We face the reality of who we are or we find ourselves caught in a lie. The stage of accepting is not only accepting of the other person, it necessitates accepting of myself, the reality of my preferences, the exposure of my weaknesses, the acknowledgement of my strengths and my desires.

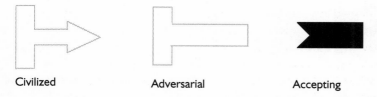

Civilized   Adversarial   Accepting

The symbol of the stage of accepting is the arrow with no head – and no base either. The movement is neither towards nor against. It is the process of letting go, of surrender, of being myself and letting you be yourself. The indent is symbolic of acceptance – accepting you into my space. Acceptance of who you are, even though that affects me. It can be a surprisingly difficult place to be in. And, like M. Scott Peck's stage of emptiness, it can feel like dying. But not the dying of becoming something I am not. Rather it is the dying of letting go.

This is not meant to imply that this is a stage or process with no conflict. True intimacy needs ways to handle conflict. This is a robust responsiveness to difference, not the wishy-washy pulling back from divergence or disagreement. Again, like the stage of emptiness, this is not the mere politically-correct tolerance of pseudo-community. It is an acceptance of who you are and who I am. In my teenage years there was a romantic poster with a quote from Fritz Perls the existential therapist, 'You are you and I am I. And if by chance we find each other, it's beautiful.' The posters did not complete the quote – and neither would I when I discovered what it was. I preferred the romance of the abbreviated version. The last line of the quote was, 'And if not it can't be helped.' Now, thirty-five years later, I agree with Fritz Perls. Back then I would have wanted to change myself, or you, so we could find each other and it would be beautiful. Now I understand the acceptance that says I have to let go changing you, and accept myself as I am – and if *then* we connect it's beautiful – and real. And if not, then changing myself or you doesn't help. It is a deeper kind of beauty. And a greater challenge.

Finding intimacy

And so the relationship comes to being intimate. The intimacy of honesty – with myself and with you. That lets you see my strengths and my weaknesses, and the places I disagree with you. That does not demand conformity. Nor that you meet my needs. It is the place of invitation. That invites you into relationship with me by being seen for who I am, warts and all – and invites – but does not demand – a response from you.

Being intimate is the characteristic of the inner circle of our relationships, the inner sacred place where relationships are a true meeting of two separate people. Often our romantic culture has implied that a coming together in intimacy is like two halves finding each other and making a whole – you meeting my needs and I meeting yours. True intimacy is a different picture. It is a coming together of two whole (though wounded) people with an acceptance of our differences and the places we do not fit. Some of us will find this in our marriages, others in close friendships or family.

Being truly intimate is a going towards the other person, not in a superficial masked way, but in openness and honesty, finding truly who I am because I am willing to self-disclose to you, as well as to receive your feedback.

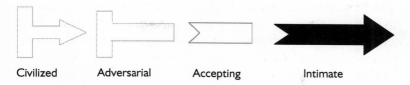

| Civilized | Adversarial | Accepting | Intimate |

The symbol includes both a going towards, and an acceptance of who you are, into me. It is the intimacy of nakedness, and the absence of shame because we both accept ourselves and the other as we are.

The stage of civility contains both towards-energy and against-energy. The adversarial stage is characterized by the against-energy of forced or manipulated influence. The stage of acceptance, in letting go of both of these, is neither towards nor against. And intimacy is a commitment to towards-energy, to accepting, even celebrating, each other's difference. The journey from civilized distance to naked intimacy requires the letting go of the need to change others, as well as the masks that hide me from others and from myself. It involves an acceptance of difference and of conflict – a learning of a way through dissimilarity and discord.

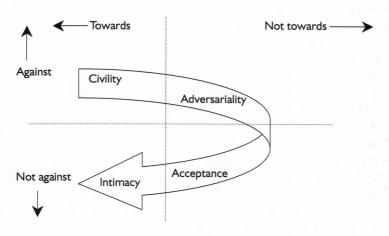

The journey from civility to intimacy

While only a few of our relationships will move right through to the stage of intimacy, the principles of relationship remain the same. Keeping our masks on will allow us to be civil but distant. Relationships will function smoothly, and will be a foundation for future possibilities. Distance may become habitual and it is likely that both people will need to desire a closer relationship for the distance to be overcome. Nevertheless the desire to make the world how we want it, and to make people after our own image, is surprisingly strong and persistent, and will propel at least some of our relationships to further nearness. The way we try to change each other is creative, diverse and often subtle, often unrecognized, even as we do it. The shift to relationship-by-invitation is essential if the relationship is going to move past this chaotic adversarial stage. Our very differences in handling these processes will often keep the relationship see-sawing back and forth between civility and adversariality – even for the length of our lives. Similarly, some relationships will see-saw between adversariality and acceptance. We will let go of the other, accepting them as they are, only to change our minds and try and convert them, or try a more subtle means of doing so. Or we will have some revelation ourselves, changing our view – and we will want our friends to change along with us. It is natural – and usually well-meaning – but some resistance is inevitable, keeping the tension of a dynamic relationship. When we face it square-on we know we do not want a friend or partner to be a clone of ourselves, a mirror image – but we often enough act as though we do. Agreeing to disagree may be one of the healthiest gifts we can give to each other. Certainly it is essential to maturity in relationships. The otherness of the other person is what enriches a relationship and causes growth in each of us. True intimacy, then, is seeing you for who you are, and accepting you anyway; seeing myself for who I am and receiving the reality of myself. And this is the way to being truly present to the other person.

❼
Being *for* the Other

How can I be truly 'present' to another person? A lot of our relationships will be task-focused, focused on mutual interest or on working towards shared goals. Even when our eyes are turned more to each other, our real focus is often ourselves, our needs, our opinions or, as we saw above, changing or influencing the other person. How are we to change this focus to a more mutual generous relationship?

The Evaluation Paradigm
An important part of the way we see ourselves, and each other, is through evaluation. We have inner criteria by which we measure each other, often unconsciously. A large part of this relates to childhood experiences. As very little children we experience our parents, or caregivers, as all-powerful. They give us our food, a safe place to live, respond to our basic needs. Most of us have experienced parents who were 'good enough' – that is, they met our needs sufficiently and provided to a reasonable extent a physically and psychologically safe world. But not unconditionally. They also taught us to conduct ourselves – socialized us – and, as we responded, gave us what we needed. This socialization process taught us what was acceptable and what wasn't, and taught us how to 'be good', to 'behave.' This socialization gave us scripts to live by – patterns that last us usually well into adulthood. All of us have scripts in our heads – often *unexamined* – whereby we monitor our own and other people's behaviour. Generally we are attracted to people who behave along similar lines, fall in with the same socialization patterns, act as we expect they should – although occasionally we may be drawn to difference, someone who seems exotic or a rebel.

Our scripts tend to go unconsidered until we run into someone who is different — or we come close to someone who at some point challenges us in a way we cannot avoid. Even then, childhood scripts, and later intentionally chosen codes of behaviour, tend to dominate our thinking, and our constant evaluation of ourselves and others. This appraisal is so pervasive that it is useful to think of it as the Evaluation Paradigm — the paradigm that has infiltrated the way our relationships function — unless we deliberately replace it with something else.

Try it

Think of someone you have noticed in the last couple of days — maybe a stranger. How much evaluation was happening? 'I like that shirt,' 'His voice is too loud,' 'She's pretty,' 'I disagree with that opinion,' 'I wish he would get out of here,' and so on.
Try to catch yourself over the next day or two — or even every hour or two — each time you look at someone. Simply notice the evaluation.

This evaluation is the basis of the shift from the civilized stage of a relationship. In the civilized stage we are 'being nice' but keeping our guard up, politely not giving voice to all the evaluation that is going on in our heads. As we get to know someone, get to be more comfortable in their presence, we are likely to let some of the evaluation slip out. At first this may be quite subtle, set in a favourable comment: 'You should come and join us next time,' 'I love that colour on you, you should wear it more often,' 'Why don't you just tell him to get off your case.' It is not that trying to influence the other person is wrong, it is that we inevitably do it from our own Evaluation Paradigm. Good relationships usually include reciprocal influence — a give and take of suggestion and response. The problem with this in the early stages of a relationship is that it is often done from *my* basis of evaluation rather than from a shared basis — or from yours.

Once we are operating out of our scripts to evaluate and change someone else we are in the adversarial stage of the relationship. Intentionally or not, we are assessing them and trying to get them to measure up to our standards – 'You should be more like me.'

I picture this as an over-against relationship, evaluating the other against my childhood scripts, or chosen 'requirements' – what I believe is required to make you (and me) an acceptable person.

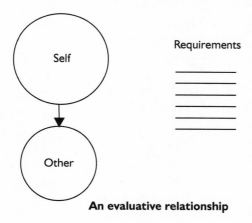

An evaluative relationship

The reality is that most of us live in this Evaluation Paradigm most of the time, not even realizing that the messages we are giving the other person are messages of critique – even when we are 'being nice'. We are, after all, 'only trying to help'. The paradigm is likely to kick in even more persistently when our roles involve any kind of hierarchy – either explicit or assumed. If I am your teacher, mentor, counsellor, older brother, team leader, 'the head of the home' or the more senior worker, we are both more likely to expect evaluation to be operating. It seems that to relate without evaluating requires intentional effort.

Noticing without evaluating

We may not even be aware that there is an alternative way to operate, or how automatically evaluation and hierarchy creep into our relationships. The problem with the Evaluation Paradigm is that valuing is implicit; we are judging the other person as wrong, immature, biased or as having no dress-sense. It is not wrong to notice difference – the damage is in the devaluing.

One of my tasks as a psychologist was to diagnose specific learning disabilities in children. Frequently parents would say to me, 'I know I shouldn't compare, but at that age his brother could read easily.' The problem is not with the comparing – how would the mother know anything was wrong if she did not make comparisons? The problem is in the valuing – or devaluing – so often implicit in the comparison. If the outcome of comparing is devaluing – that is when the harm is done. 'He can't do what his brother does, so he is lazy, stupid, uncooperative.' The judgement is the destructive part – not the noticing of difference.

Choosing to step out of the Evaluation Paradigm takes intentional action. To deliberately shift from an 'above' or 'below' position to a 'side-by-side' one involves a conscious choice for most of us.

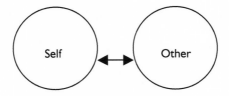

A side-by-side relationship

In stepping into this role I purposefully let go of my own superiority, expertise and certainty of opinions and invite your perspective, not in order to change you but to understand and accept you – to see the world as you see it. I make myself equal with you, recognizing that we are walking the journey of life together, side-by-side, learning as we travel.

The other big change is that the requirements list is removed from our interaction. This is not done easily. I cannot just pretend it is not there – it is, after all, woven into my way of perceiving the world. Instead of trying to ignore it I need to acknowledge it, see it for what it is – My Scripts – and choose to put it aside, or hold it lightly for the time being. 'For the time being' because it will return whether I want it to or not – it is part of how I make sense of the world, how I interpret life.

But for now I choose to put my scripts and requirements aside, and to enter the other person's world, attempting to understand the requirements they live by, the sometimes tyrannical scripts that energize their behaviour. And there *is* energy in our scripts, they seem to have a life of their own, propelling us to conform and meet our internal standards – or suffer the consequence of internal criticism, even flagellation. The other person has their own scripts and trying to inflict my own on them is often counter-productive, met by resistance. Listening to their perspectives, their internal evaluations, is a much more profitable exercise. Any lasting change a person is likely to make will be in line with their own scripts, or will necessitate an intentional choice of change to those internal requirements. The best I can give another person is often to be beside them as they examine their own faulty scripts and decide themselves where they might change them.

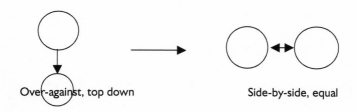

Over-against, top down   Side-by-side, equal

The movement from an over-against, top-down position to a side-by-side relationship is often more difficult than it seems. This is because it involves a letting go of our own way of understanding the world. For many people this is surprisingly challenging, even scary.

Try it

Think of someone with whom you have a satisfying relationship.

How much of their way of seeing the world do you understand? Is there a sense of being side by side? If so, how have you achieved this? If not, who is in the superior position? What would it be like if the relationship was more equal?

Now think of a relationship where there is some tension. What would it be like to let go your way of seeing things, to accept the other person's perspective? Most of us at this point find the difficulty – the belief, or opinion or value that we don't want to let go. How can I hold my value or attitude in one hand, but enter into the person's way of seeing things with the other? This may involve specifically asking them their viewpoint.

A heart towards

One of the ways I conceptualize this process of choosing the side-by-side position is to think about it as having 'my heart towards' the other person. I don't have to agree with everything, I may in fact be very different, but if 'my heart is towards' them it makes all the difference to how I see them and to how the relationship operates. Having my heart towards someone is choosing to be *for* them, choosing to care what life is like for them, and wanting to do them good. This often takes quite a lot of internal work. If my colleague has just disagreed with me *again*, my natural reaction is to either withdraw, or react – correct, confront – even hurt or make a sarcastic comment. To take the time to look for the good, to choose to value the person and the relationship, to try and see from his point of view, to want for him what he wants, to see the best in him – all take energy and a choice for a good long-term outcome. And whether I know it or not, it is likely that my colleague will intuit my underlying response – whether 'my heart is towards' him or not.

I remember one such incident. I was in a meeting where I needed to ask for some resources for my department. A colleague cut across my request, minimizing it. The meeting continued but I left it seething. I thought of a number of cutting and sarcastic things I could say – ways to tell her what I thought of her behaviour. I played over possible scenarios. But I was determined to practice what I am preaching, to do the internal work necessary to respond to her from a side-by-side position. I decided I needed to talk about what had happened, explaining my own frustration about resources and hurt at her behaviour. Eventually I suggested a cup of coffee – my panacea for everything. We chatted and I then brought up the incident, explaining a little of my point of view. Obviously she too, had been doing some internal revising. She quickly assured me that she was on my side. The whole dynamic changed. I am convinced that my choice to turn my heart towards her enabled her to take a conciliatory position. Maybe her internal work allowed me to let go of my anger! Whatever the mystery below the surface, the result was that our relationship is closer and more open than before the incident occurred.

Assertiveness

Doing the internal work is the key to assertiveness. Being assertive is not the same as being passive, or being walked over. Nor is it being aggressive. Being assertive is stating my experience, my desire, my boundaries, without intruding on those of the other. Being aggressive is pushing what I want, what I believe, without making space for the other. And being passive is stepping back from my boundaries, letting the other person's view dominate or prevail. Being assertive means being able to declare what I want, but owning that, giving room for the other person to do likewise – and in my heart giving them permission and freedom to do so. Sometimes being assertive does not take many words, but is the stance I take, an internal honesty and willingness to be open if necessary.

The difference between a passive stance, an aggressive one and an assertive one are shown below. The first scenario is a request for time off work, the second is a wish to visit family. The passive position is a weak statement of preference with deferral implicit. The aggressive position is a demand for what I want and a refusal of the other's disagreement. An assertive position is a clear statement of preference with room for the other to make their own choice of response.

Passive	Aggressive	Assertive
I wish I could have some time off for a break.	We work far too long hours around here, and you need to take note of your workers' needs. I'm taking tomorrow off, and if you don't like it you can sack me.	I'm finding that I am exhausted and not working at my best. I need to take a day off to recoup.
I wonder if we could go and visit my family, but only if you want to.	We're always spending time with *your* friends, doing what *you* want. Now you can fit in with what *I* want and visit my family.	I really want to spend some time with my family. I'd like it if you would come too.

Sometimes being assertive involves a willingness to take the consequences of the other person's disagreement. This can be challenging if it is perceived that the other person has more power. I may have to choose between my own priorities. However, bringing this out into the open, letting the other person see my dilemma, and choosing to be on side with them can change the dynamic of how the decision is made.

My position and attitude are often very influential in the response of the other person. The passive position, like that of the compliant, invites the other person to overrule. I give the message that what you want is more important than what I want – and you respond accordingly. Unless you too are passive – and then there is a competition to defer the most! 'No, what do *you* want?' No, no, what do *you* want?' 'No, it's your choice.' 'No, really, I don't mind' and so on. The passive person finds assertiveness challenging because their internal scripts have taught them that being nice is how you get love. Stating what I want feels like a risk of losing the relationship. In the end the passive person has to choose between real relationships and the false ones of constant deferral.

An aggressive position often invites an aggressive response. In fact, an aggressive position tends to give the other person only two choices of response – to defer and go along with the aggressive person, or to take an aggressive stand in reply. The aggressive person is giving the message 'Give me want I want or else.' Often they pair up with someone who gives them what they want – but who may ultimately choose the 'Or else', and then the relationship founders. An aggressive person often finds himself in trouble in a number of relationships, and tends to draw strong reactions to eventually curb his own. For the aggressive person to learn to be assertive often feels very challenging – it feels as though they are giving away power, risking being dominated. Letting the relationship be broken can be a preferred option to the fear of helplessness.

Being assertive takes both internal work and practice. The internal work is facing the fear of losing the relationship (for the passive person), or the fear of powerlessness (for the aggressive person). And practice is simply that – stating what I want clearly and without manipulation – over and over.

Try it

Think of a situation where you are not getting what you want, what you need. Put into words what it is that you want – this might be surprisingly difficult – but an obvious necessary first step. State how the present position is affecting you – I am tired, I am not working well, I have family expectations I feel obliged to respond to. (When you actually talk to the other person you may not actually voice this – but it is important that you at least acknowledge it to yourself.) Practice stating your preference – out walking, in front of a mirror, or to a trusted friend.

If what you have chosen is too hard to begin with choose something less important to experiment with. Or a less important relationship – the girl on the checkout, or someone you won't see again! Practicing assertiveness really does make it come more easily. It may also help to put into words how you

think the position is for the other person. This is usually best
done tentatively. 'I know it's important to you that this project
succeeds, and I'm wondering if you're concerned it won't get
done if I take some time off.'

The most important thing for assertiveness to work in a
relationship is that your heart is *for* the other person. It is easy to
make the focus what I want, or to stumble over saying the words
in the right way – but truly being *for* the other person allows them
to intuit that I am not trying to make life difficult for them, or to
go against what they want.

Changing the way you relate to someone else – becoming more
assertive, less aggressive or less passive – can take time – from both
sides of the relationship. Harriet Lerner – has written a number
of books, including *Dance of Connection*,[13] where she likens close
relationships to a dance. In any close relationship we are used to
how the other person behaves, we 'know the dance steps', and
if you suddenly change your step I try to get you back into step
by sticking solidly to mine. It can feel sometimes as though a
relationship is impossible to change because of this dynamic.
Persisting in assertive behaviour is important. Sometimes, explaining
the change to the other person is the only way forward.

Turning towards – a full bank account

Being *for* the other person is not a one-time decision. It is worked
out in ordinary everyday relationships – during tiredness, pressure
and mundane everyday life. It is a conscious choice to be responsive
to the other person and their needs.

John and Julie Gottman have researched successful marriage for
the last twenty years by videotaping couple's conversations and
interactions – and finding out what actions are predictably part
of long-lasting marriages. One of the major principles they have
isolated is the willingness of couples to 'turn towards' each other.
They liken this turning towards – the everyday little actions of
listening to each other, responding to each other's wants, discussing

each other's ideas – as money in an emotional bank account. 'They are building up emotional savings that can serve as a cushion when times get rough, when they're faced with a major life stress or conflict. Because they have stored up all of this goodwill, they are better able to make allowances for each other when a conflict arises. They can maintain a positive sense of each other and their marriage even during hard times.'[14]

Our natural reaction to irritation, to mistakes, to conflict, is negative. Creating long term healthy relationships depends on choices to be *for* the other person – especially in the context of the negatives. This does not mean being passive, being a doormat – rather it is a heart choice for the other person and for the relationship. The Gottmans have likened this to a healthy bank balance. Another metaphor is that of a bridge – a bridge that holds the two people together so that the traffic of their interactions can continue to flow back and forth.

The relationship as a bridge

I remember once thinking about how I should talk to someone about a certain issue. I knew I needed to tiptoe in – as though wearing ballet shoes – to find my way among the eggshells. And it felt as though I was wearing big work boots that would be sure to break whatever I stepped on. I remember thinking that I was just going to have to take the risk and trust the relationship to take my weight.

A new relationship is like a bridge in construction – or maybe a rope thrown across a chasm. At first it is fragile. Saying the wrong thing could mean it doesn't survive. Over the years our long-term relationships get strengthened. They become like strongly reinforced concrete bridges. Bridges we can walk on with all our weight.

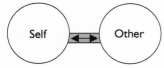

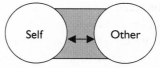

New or more distant relationship   Well-established or closer relationship

Remember the mother–child interaction described in Chapter One? The mother looks away and the baby feels disconnected. Slowly he learns that even if she is not in the room she still exists. He has a sense of the relationship even when the other person is not immediately present. As he weathers some 'winters' in his relationship he learns that spring always comes, that his mother will be there for him, that the relationship will weather the storm.

As our relationships continue over time, as we survive some winters, enjoy some summers, the bridge is reinforced. We can say some things, risk some self-disclosure we would not have done earlier. Our self-disclosure and feedback hopefully strengthen the bridge. Sometimes something happens that pulls away one of the supports and the bridge is weakened. We need time to build the relationship again, reassuring the other person of our trustworthiness, our heart *for* them. If they have a history of betrayal, or if we have hurt them too often already, the rebuilding may take some time.

Sometimes a disagreement may be so bad that the bridge itself is threatened. Rather than focusing on what the disagreement is about the bridge itself might need some focus for a period of time. Some reassurances, some demonstrations of concern, of trustworthiness, some vulnerability. When someone is hurting they can do serious damage to the relationship, like throwing hand grenades, or sawing through cables. Insisting on discussing a difficult topic at times like this may be like trying to drive a truck over a matchwood bridge. Better to back off and build the bridge. Backing off and waiting may be helpful, but time alone does not heal. Time just gives space for some healing work to be done.

Talking about the relationship can be delicate – but it also can be a good way to build the bridge.

8
Talking About Relationships

Talking about relationships is awkward for most of us. Most of us were not brought up in families who could talk openly about what was happening between us in a way that gave each other freedom. It is usually in our families where it is most difficult to make the boundary statements, 'When you do that, I feel...'. We have usually worked out ways that the family functions and we stick to our patterns, not wanting to rock the boat. Or we withdraw into other relationships and establish another way of being in a separate context. We may then return to our family and try to change them to fit with who we have become. Talking about the dynamic is often outside of our experience and comfort zone.

Using labels constructively
One of the easiest ways to talk about relationships is to use labels. 'I'm a Sanguine and you're a Phlegmatic.' 'You're an extrovert and I'm an introvert.' 'I have a Greek grandfather so I tend to be argumentative.' 'My British inheritance has meant I keep a stiff upper lip, never showing my feelings.' All labels stereotype, simplifying complex human beings and their interactions. As a result they make us less than who we are. But sometimes they are a first step to understanding difference. And they can be a less threatening way to talk about difference because we can talk without implied Rightness and Wrongness. They are a way of noticing difference without getting caught in the judgement of the Evaluation Paradigm. Being an extrovert doesn't make me better than you, just different.

The reality is that most of us behave in certain reasonably consistent patterns – at least in a particular context. It is sometimes helpful to differentiate between contexts when generalizing about behaviour patterns. 'I am an extrovert in my work because that is what the job requires, but when I get home I need to re-energize alone – and so I am quite an introvert.' The point of using labels is to explain ourselves to each other, to give us language to understand each other's worlds.

Another reason to label patterns of behaviour is to acknowledge them, and so *free ourselves from them*. One psychologist explained 'I don't put people into boxes, but I keep finding them there.' On one occasion when I taught personality I gave everyone in the class a little box to remind them 'Understanding yourself helps you jump *out* of the box.' The fact is that we do tend to get into habit patterns of behaviour, and certain contexts will call out certain patterns. Recognizing these, even labelling them, can give me the freedom to change my behaviour, to choose *not* to follow my usual pattern, to change how I interact.

There are many different ways to assess and label personality. I have not included these as they can be found elsewhere – on the Web or in books – but I have included a few comparisons to give some language to talk about our interactions and differences. Of course the reality is that each person is unique and will 'do relationships' differently from every other person. Any talk of relationship is necessarily generalizing, and therefore doesn't fit everyone all the time.

Inner and outer worlds

One of the distinctions already referred to is between extroverts, those who prefer to live in the exterior world, and introverts, those who prefer the inner world inside their own heads or feelings. The fact is that we all live in both an inner world *and* an outer world. It is a matter of inclination which of these is our preferred space. To clarify this idea of 'both-and' along with preference, try signing your name in your usual way. It is easy, natural, automatic, smooth. Now sign your name with the other hand. For most of us it is awkward, unnatural, jerky and needs concentration. It is not that we cannot sign with our non-preferred hand. For some of us it may even be relatively easy – and certainly decipherable enough to use to withdraw money from a bank. It is a bit like this with our inner and outer worlds. We all live in both – but introverts prefer their own world, and tend to relate to the outer world a little awkwardly, needing time to think and respond. Extroverts, on the other hand, are often smooth operators in the outside world; they think on their feet, and don't understand why the rest of us need time to think about what we are going to say. Their awkwardness is more in their internal world, where they may be less adept at knowing what they feel or think – they might even have to talk about it to find out.

Relating to an extreme extrovert is very different from relating to a reclusive introvert. The latter needs time and space, time alone, time to think and respond – and a safe context to open up. Extroverts enjoy the give and take of relationship and are stimulated by discussion and action and energized by people – and for some, the more the better. Generally they find introverts rather frustrating (apart from the fact that introverts give them more space to tell their stories), and want introverts to give them some clues as to what is going on in their inner world.

Of course, as in every other distinction between people, there are all sorts of points along the continuum. Most people can switch from their inner world to the outer one, and vice versa. Preference is about where they spend the most time, the most comfortably. Understanding this basic difference between people can help me give space to people's preferences, preferred ways of being – and give me language to talk about it.

Try it

Think of a particular context – your work, a certain group of friends or your home.

Do you tend to be extrovert or introvert in that context?

Are you more reflective, tuning into your own thoughts and feelings; or are you tending to instigate relationship, initiating interaction, or entertaining?

Are you choosing to work or relax alone, refuelling in your own space; or are you finding a group of people to interact with, and draw energy from?

Are you aware of your own feelings or thoughts, thinking through what you will say or express, or are you quick to talk, working out what you'll say as you go?

Transactional analysis

In Chapter Five the roles of parent, adult and child were explored. The language and categories of transactional analysis are a useful way to talk about relationships and to interpret interactions between people. This present chapter is less about roles that people take than about their natural and easiest way of functioning and therefore interacting with each other.

Head, heart and action

Another way to recognize difference is to see people's preference for head, heart or action. People of the heart tend to come towards you, that is, you experience them as warm, accepting, wanting to be liked, wanting to be admired. They tend to easily find the good in others before they criticize. They want to be in a relationship, they want you to respond to them. Sometimes of course, this can feel like too much warmth, or sweetness or niceness, and our natural reaction may be to back off. But usually these are the people who want to make friends, who want to include others, who show you their artwork, their home, their writing, or inside their heads – and hearts. They feel for you and want to make you feel better, or at least feel with them, feel the depth of love, hurt, anguish that they experience. These are the natural 'people-people', the ones who end up in jobs as teachers, in the caring professions, or expressing feelings – artists and actors.

People of the heart are predisposed to to draw us into a relationship, to make us feel and respond. It is usually reasonably easy to come into a relationship with people of the heart; the difficulty is finding the boundaries and the appropriate distance. And their difficulty is that they often give too much of themselves, are seen as a bleeding heart, have difficulty defining where they end and the other begins.

People of the head are naturally more detached. They may enjoy relationships, even instigate family gatherings and parties, but you can feel below the surface that they have their guard up. They are more likely to be analyzing, or in some way processing, what is going on. They are wary of too much emotion, especially pain, sadness or anger. Being in relationship with people who prefer to be in their heads means that they probably will not easily talk about real feelings, not as they are happening, at least. The world of these people is made safer by keeping feelings reserved, and relationships are more likely to have a slightly distant feel about them. In contrast to the towards-energy of the heart people, head people have an away-energy − a slight stepping back, a holding at arm's length. Head people don't mind being in the civilized stages of relationships. They may even like the idea of emptiness that Scott Peck talks about (Chapter Five) − so long as it is not followed by too close a community afterwards!

Some head people are actually active in relationship building − but it tends to be only with those they consider 'insiders.' They are willing to be in a relationship with people they consider 'safe' and protect themselves from other relationships by positioning themselves in some kind of structured or recognised in-group. It is the 'outsiders' who are aware of the distancing of these people, while the insiders can feel included, but in some way expected to behave in the correct way.

The third group of people in this scheme is people of action. These people want change. They tend to react almost without thinking or feeling first − and therefore are sometimes called people of the gut − the gut reaction. These are people who see what's wrong and want to change it. This is an against-energy, an energy that comes from reaction and critique. It is easily found in the adversarial stage discussed in the last chapter, and indeed action people may be happy to stay in this stage in most of their relationships – often to the discomfort of those around them! It is more difficult to be in a relationship with this group of people because we will often enough be the focus of their energy. Sometimes what this group wants more than anything is reaction in return. Some of them enjoy provocation and don't understand that the rest of us find it difficult.

Somewhat paradoxically, there are some people in the action category who look the least active of all – until they are interested in something and then their energy doesn't stop. Their against-energy is more subtle – they tend to be passive aggressive. If they disagree they simply disappear. They are people of action because, first, their gut reaction drives them to respond – against or in withdrawal – and because they *act* on what is happening rather than processing in their heads or expressing their emotions.

Recognizing ourselves and others as predominantly heart, head or action can help us understand the different energy systems operating, and the pull into or out of relationship. The important thing in recognizing these patterns is to enable us to value the individual person and so to be able to respect their pattern but not be compelled to disregard our own preferences and boundaries in response.

One good friendship I have is with a person who has a lot of against energy. She has high standards and high expectations of herself and therefore also of those around her. On occasion we have had to work closely and I have known the discomfort of her criticism against me or other people. We have been able to talk about the differences between us because of understanding these concepts. Our relationship necessitates a lot of coffee, but we have become close as a result – the outcomes, and the internal work thus stimulated, are worth the process.

Try it

Think about a few people you know well. Try to identify whether they operate predominantly from head, heart or action. Notice whether there is a towards-, away-from, or an against-energy.

Think of someone you feel easily drawn to – do they have a towards-energy? Or is the attraction more about similarities between you?

Which of head, heart or action do you notice most in yourself?

Head, heart and action – in me

Differentiating between heart, head and action has another application. In the same way that we all have an inner world and an outer world, we all have head, heart and action within us. While we tend to prefer one of these and so 'live' in this space, we are all people of several parts, which constantly interact but don't always work together as a whole.

The head is the place of our thoughts, concepts and words, our knowledge and ideas about the world and people, our education, our reading, our beliefs, our analysis. Some people have very carefully thought-through ideas and belief systems which are consistent and conceptualized to an overall 'worldview' – a framework for understanding their world in terms of truth, right and wrong and being. Most people are more likely to have millions of facts and ideas stored as they might in their spare-cupboard-that-holds-everything – or a computer with no separate files or folders. Ask them something and they can tell you a fact, or what their teacher said, or what their old grandfather used to say, but it is not necessarily consistent with everything else they know or believe. One of the goals of education is to teach us 'how to think', to form a more whole view and consistent understanding.

Whether we have a consistent philosophy which can be articulated rationally, or whether we have a 'spare-cupboard' arrangement, we will live according to our thought patterns and beliefs, however mistaken or misinformed they are. The story of Mrs Smith, who believed the 'fact' that her mother had died, and reacted accordingly shows how our emotions and behaviour are influenced by our knowledge and beliefs – whether faulty or not.

In relationships our thoughts and beliefs are often faulty. We have gathered our ideas piecemeal, through experiences, education, television shows – true to life or Hollywood versions. Most of us do not learn about relationships and communication in a formal way, it is part of our socialization and our culture. Much of what goes on in our heads is 'common knowledge' and we assume that other people think in a similar way that we do. The multiculturalization of our cities and communities is bringing some of the 'common knowledge' into question. There is a small town in Canada – Herouxville, Quebec – which has just published regulations against beating women to death and burning them alive.[15] An unnecessary regulation, we might think. Their point is that there is so much immigration there that they want to make it very clear what is acceptable – what is the 'common knowledge' of their community'. 'Come and live with us,' they say, 'but there are a few ground rules you need to know and accept. We don't mind what colour, what culture, what sexual orientation you have, you are welcome, but don't bring these destructive parts of your culture with you.'

As any of us who have married or are in committed relationships know, there are differences in our 'common knowledge'. And what I considered that 'everyone knows' is different, in places, for you. The point is that for relationships to work well, we need to let each other into our heads. I need to tell you about my beliefs, my way of making sense of the world, my expectations of behaviour. And I need to listen to your perceptions, to try and see through your eyes, not dismissing the differences as 'your weird ideas'. We need to practice sharing what is 'in our heads'.

Head, heart and action in our relationships

In my experience numbers of marriages founder because one person thinks the other person knows what they want and is choosing not to respond. 'Have you told him this is what is happening for you?' 'I told him, weeks ago.' 'Could you tell him again?' We somehow think that what is in my head – what I 'know' – is 'common knowledge.' Sometimes we have to 'act out' what is inside our heads so the other person sees it.

Years ago a friend explained to me the need for a marriage to have a 'false bottom'. She said that marriages often break up because one partner tries and tries to get the other to hear them, and finally gives up and walks away – only to find that *now* the partner wants to understand. She pointed out that one partner – usually the woman, but by no means always – is unhappy and tries to tell her partner. The partner doesn't take a lot of notice – not knowing what to do, assuming it will pass, thinking it's just a phase. She tells him again. He still doesn't know how to respond, thinks she's being emotional maybe, hopes things will improve, maybe even tries to change for a while. She brings it up again. The same thing happens. Or maybe he reacts in anger or picks on something he doesn't like about her. She begins to grieve the loss of her hopes. She gives up telling him. He thinks things have improved. She grieves, talks to her girlfriends, begins to think of other possibilities for her life. Maybe another man comes into the picture, or an opportunity to take a job, just as her children are growing up. She leaves, her grieving largely done. And finally he realizes how serious it all was for her. He tries to win her back. It's too late, her grieving is done, her energy is elsewhere. 'But I *told* you,' she says.

I have met men who have been through this scenario. They still don't know why she didn't tell them sooner. The 'false bottom' my friend was talking about, was a demonstration of the unhappiness *before* the grieving goes too far. It is very hard to reconnect when the grieving has been done. The person who is hurting needs to find a way to let the other person know how bad it is for them. 'Telling him' often isn't enough. Packing up and leaving for a time might actually help as long as it is done with the intention of finding ways to work on the relationship. Acting out what is going on inside my head is often necessary to communicate strongly enough, together with doing the hard work of thinking through what the specific things are that we need to work on, specifically, how do I need things done differently so that this relationship is working for me?

The first step, then, is to tell you what is going on inside my head, to share with you my ideas and beliefs and how the world is for me. This is an important part of intimacy and being known for who I am. But I need to be aware that relationships are also about actions – and my friend, my partner, will believe my actions more than my words. If I am still cooking the meals, being polite, having sex, how does my partner know that my words – especially from months ago – are still true?

There is a fun little exercise our counselling students do. Try saying something in words, but set your body and face to say the opposite. 'That is so interesting', said with body leaning away, arms folded, bored expression. 'No everything is just fine,' said with hunched shoulders, gloomy face, arms crossed. 'No, I'm not angry at all,' said with gritted teeth, set jaw, looming posture. When words and actions are in opposition we simply do not believe the words.

So how do we make our bodies, our actions, communicate what we want them to? The most important thing is the internal work. Most of us are not good actors. Even if our acting is very good, we can maybe fool most of the people most of the time, but by no means all of the people all of the time. The mask wears thin. It seems that most of us are not designed to lie well.

Yet to complicate matters, we easily believe what we *want* to believe or expect to believe. If you assure me that things are fine, even though your body is blatantly saying the opposite, if I want to believe you I can easily be tricked by your words. We often don't hear what the other person says because we *expect* them to be saying something else.

Parts of me at odds

The challenge is to line up my words with my actions – this is authenticity. Being authentic is having inner world and outer world in sync. The reality is that we are often ambivalent – we think or feel two different things at the same time – we do want to go, but we don't want to go. Part of me wants this, but another part of me wants that. One of the common Gestalt counselling exercises highlights this. It is the Two Chair method, and it lets me experience the two parts of myself as separate. Often we are stuck because one part works against the other, not allowing me to act on either. In the Two Chair method I clarify the two different parts, thoughts, wishes. I sit in one chair and voice my wish to leave my work, start studying, do something different with my life. Then I sit in the other chair and talk about my fear of change, my insecurity about giving up my job, my uncertainty about being able to change. As I physically sit in a different chair I am able to express what I really want or feel, knowing that the other chair, the other part of me, still exists, and will have a chance to be heard. Often this process helps me clarify my desires and my fears, and helps me find a way forward.

We may find that we are communicating one part of us, one set of ideas or preferences, in one relationship, and another part in a different relationship. Most of us can't sustain this kind of contradiction indefinitely and something has to give. Finding a safe person to talk about the contradictions, the different sides of myself, can help me move beyond the stuck place and into more authenticity in my relationships. Sometimes the contradiction is because one part of us is giving too much power to another person. When I am at home I feel obliged to go along with my parents' beliefs and expectations. While this might keep the peace in the short term, or maintain an important relationship for a period of time, it is generally not healthy in the long run – and certainly does not make for an intimate relationship.

It may be a matter of boundaries – owning my own beliefs, ideas and attitudes. Sometimes we need a period of time to formulate our ideas, our changing beliefs, and exposing them to criticism too early on is too risky. In that case we may need time – and we can practice articulating our ideas with safe people so that we can express them even in the face of opposition.

Most of us have most difficulty in sharing new ideas or beliefs with our parents and we are particularly sensitive to the probability of their disagreement. Having grown up with our parents as our authority figures, it is very difficult to change the dynamic of the relationship so that we do not give authority in a way that is no longer appropriate. Of course, in some cultures, the giving of authority to parents is expected to last a lifetime. The cost is intimacy; authenticity in the relationship.

Authority in relationships can be very subtle. It seems to remain in relationships long after its initial purpose is over. Authority begins by the choice to defer to the other person. In many relationships this is appropriate – parent, teacher, mentor, leader, manager, expert. The other knows more than I do, or has legitimate power in my life. Or maybe I place them on a pedestal for some emotional reason, or out of admiration. So I defer. However, I grow up, I learn more, I develop my own beliefs, I step out of the organizational role. My tendency is to continue to defer to the other person. This is a giving away of power, and a power imbalance in relationships makes for a different kind of relationship than one with equal power. It is unlikely that you will truly know what I think if you are in a power relationship with me. It is likely that, to some extent at least, I will be saying what I think you want to hear.

The effect of a power imbalance is that we lose our voice. I feel as though I cannot say what I want to. I say things in a weaker way, or I prevaricate, hesitate or evade the issue. We tend to be very sensitive to power and find it much more difficult to speak openly to a person in a position of power as we would if they were not in that position. If, on the other hand, I am the one with power, it can *feel* to me as though I am giving the other person space to be honest. It is hard for us to believe the effect of our power on the other person. This issue needs to be talked about openly if there is to be any hope of openness from both sides of the power relationship. It is as though one part of me is still deferring to the other person – even while another part of me is now adult, disengaged, knowledgeable.

One of the most powerful ways to help a person change is to look with them at the contradictions within themselves. The messages of the words, and the messages of the actions. 'On one hand you are telling me that you want to leave, but your actions are showing your choice to stay. What's that like for you?' 'You are saying that you want to spend time with me. I've noticed that for the last two weeks you've been too busy. Do you want to talk about what's happening?' Noticing the contradictions without accusing the other person makes a space to talk about the contradictory messages, the different parts of the person. Trying to make a person change from the outside is usually ineffective, but looking at contradictions within a person can free them to move beyond a place of being stuck.

Communicating about emotions

Tuning in to the differences between our words and our actions is one way of noticing contradictions. Another way is to notice our emotions. Some people are hardly aware of their emotions, while others' lives are dominated by them. Emotions in themselves are not right or wrong, good or bad – but they are motivators for our behaviours and a huge influence in our experience of how our life is. In Chapter Three we explored how to own our own feelings. The focus here is to be aware of feelings and where they may be at odds with what we believe or how we are acting.

Again, we may pick up on someone else's emotion even when they are not disclosing it directly. If I am angry with you or critical of you, usually you will pick up the signs however much I am trying to disguise it. Bringing the emotion, or at least the cause of it, may be useful. Noticing the signs without accusing is an important part of being able to discuss the issue objectively. Saying 'You're acting as though you are mad at me,' will easily sound like an accusation. Owning my own perception would enable me to say, more mildly, 'I'm wondering if I have done something to upset you.' Or, 'I'm feeling some distance between us, can we talk about that?' Or, 'We haven't seemed so close lately. I'm concerned about that, and I'm wondering if there is something I can do.'

The complication of emotions in relationships is that I bring my own history into every relationship. I can easily interpret someone else's behaviour as rejection if I have a history of rejection. I can easily interpret comment as criticism if my history has formed in me a self-critical attitude. I look at the world through my own emotional glasses, and the only way to know whether I am accurate in my perception is to be able to have other people to check with. Of course they bring their history – but between us we may be closer to the reality!

In a relationship it is often helpful to know whether an emotion is my 'stuff', my unresolved history. Thinking about it doesn't work too well, but the emotion itself can take us to the root.

Try it

You need to be feeling an emotion to work through this process. Remembering a recent incident where you reacted strongly may be a way to return to the emotion. Once you are feeling it, stay there, sit with it. Try and describe what it feels like. Consider where it may be in your body – tension in your shoulders, a knot in the stomach, tightness across the chest, an ache in your heart. Think about what colour or shape it might be.

When you are in touch with the emotion ask yourself, 'When have I felt like this before?' This is not a 'head' question. It is a body or feeling question. Your emotion will lead you back to an earlier incident much more accurately than your head can.

Recently I was visiting my older brother at his work. As we left his office, he with his arms full, I picked up his briefcase. It immediately took me back to an incident I hadn't thought of in decades. When he was at high school and I was an admiring nine-year-old I would sometimes walk to the street corner to meet him – and carry his school bag. The physical action of picking up his bag reminded me of an incident forty-five years earlier. Our body actions and emotions can often connect us back to childhood events in a different way from our usual memory process.

Reconnecting with a childhood memory of pain, rejection

or anger can often help us understand the intensity of a present emotion. Having operated as more of a head person than a heart person, I have only learned this process slowly. Previously, if I over-reacted to something someone said or did, I would dismiss the emotion, telling myself not to be silly. Now I am more likely to notice the emotion, not necessarily in the midst of an interchange, but a little later when I have some space to process. 'I was really angry about that.' 'That comment really hurt me.' Rather than minimizing what I have felt, 'He didn't really mean it', 'I should just forget it, I'm over-reacting', I now stay with the emotion. 'What is this really about?', I will ask myself. 'What other incident does it remind me of?'

Sometimes it will be a current incident that is fuelling my reaction. When my marriage was breaking up I would find myself furious with bank tellers, checkout operators, truck drivers. I would slow down, stay with my anger and ask myself what it was about. Usually it was about not being listened to, feeling as though I was not being considered – and of course the source was my marriage. That was where the work needed to be done, rather than in telling the bank teller what I thought of her bank in the heat of the moment.

Often our over-reactions will stem from childhood. It's easy to understand why a woman who was sexually abused by her father and her uncle should hate all men. The work needed to change the effect of childhood trauma is usually profound. For many of us though, it is much smaller, and seemingly insignificant, incidents that lie in our memories. It is as though our childhood experiences tell us what the world is like and we carry that belief, magnifying it into adult situations, almost like the hard wiring in a computer. An incident where my husband laughs at me, playfully, can really sting. If I sit with the emotion it brings to mind – being laughed at as a child, and the humiliation of that incident – staying with the emotion, telling my partner of the original incident, then being reassured and held by him in the present can bring healing to the past event.

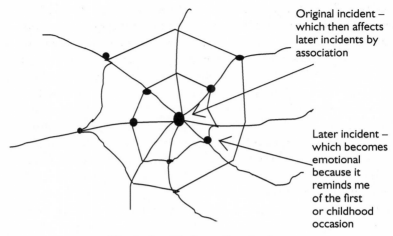

Original incident –
which then affects
later incidents by
association

Later incident –
which becomes
emotional
because it
reminds me
of the first
or childhood
occasion

The 'cobweb' of emotional pain

This is sometimes called inner healing or healing of the memories. It is not a forgetting of the past, but rather a reconnecting with a past memory in order to heal the pain of it, thus defusing the intensity of the emotion, which we otherwise bring into our present interactions and relationships. This process is not an intellectual one. We have to reconnect with the feeling. It is in the experience of the emotion, and the memory, that the healing can come. Thus our present relationships come to be about the present rather than being infused with the hurt, anger, and rejection of the past.

Expressing love

Expressing love is a very important part of learning to express emotion and commitment, and tends to come naturally as head, heart or action. Relationships can founder on differences of expression of love between people – the experience of not being loved because my partner, or parents, or friends, express love in a different way from how I long for it. Again, some broad categories can help us understand ourselves, and each other.

Gary Chapman, a marriage counsellor with decades of experience, describes different ways of communicating and receiving love in *The Five Love Languages*.[16] He believes that most people experience love primarily in one of five ways – physical touch, words of affirmation, quality time, acts of service and gift-giving. If my partner likes to express love by physical touch – holding hands, back-rubs, sex – and I prefer words of affirmation – hearing the words 'I love you', compliments, cards with thoughtful communication – we won't hear each other. Or if my love language is acts of service and my partner loves to buy me gifts, but never thinks to help with the dishes, fix the broken appliance, or run the children to their sports practice, I will feel unloved, however much money was spent. Or if my partner does all of these but I am longing for quality time – a deep and meaningful over coffee, or special time together – I still won't feel loved.

It is natural that we express our love in the way we want to receive it, but if our love language is not the same as our partner's we will miss each other. At first it can feel unnatural to write loving words in a card when we'd rather just give a hug to express our affection – or awkward to buy a gift when we would rather do something helpful – but the energy is wasted if the other person doesn't receive the love intended.

Try it

Think of how you express yourself to people you love. What kinds of things do you tend to do, or wish you could do, to show your love to people?
When do you feel most loved? What is it that you find yourself looking forward to, or wishing those you love would do for you?
Try to put into words what you prefer in terms of love being expressed to you.

Using labels and people's classification systems helps us to talk about ourselves. However, it necessarily simplifies the complexity of who we are. Labelling needs particular caution when we are applying it to other people. Because it is reductionistic, it can feel to the other person as though we do not see the richness of who they are. It should only be used to help understanding, and to therefore give freedom to the person to be who they choose to be.

Types, systems and 'languages' are ways of giving each other information about ourselves. They can help us find a way to be more comfortable talking about differences. In the end though, for true intimacy we need to be personal. 'This is what I like.' 'This is my preference.' 'When you do that I feel this.' These are surprisingly challenging statements.

What is it that makes talking like this so challenging? It comes back to our inner scripts, our acceptability and our ways of protecting ourselves.

❾
Influencing Others

Kinds of influence

Relationships with others usually involve influence in one, or both directions. Sometimes our roles are focused on influencing – teaching, selling, consulting, parenting and so on. In friendship, relationship influence is more often two-way and seems to work best if there is an agreement to accept or reject the influence of the other person as we feel is appropriate. If a friend is always telling me what to do and I feel I will offend her if I refuse, it is unlikely our friendship will last. On the other hand, most intimate relationships will include reciprocal influence and a willingness to listen to each other's ideas and be affected by them. While some relationships may start as one-way relationships, such as parenting or teaching, the relationships which become deep and lasting are those which allow influence in either direction. Parents who allow their children to teach them, or discuss decisions with them, teachers who listen to their students' experiences and adapt their teaching accordingly, are the ones who develop adult to adult relationships with their maturing children and students.

Kinds of influence can be understood in the terms of head, heart and action already discussed. To influence someone from a 'head' position is to use reason, facts, understanding of ideas, expertise. Heart influence is to stir the emotions, to inspire, challenge, anger, or to arouse pity. Action focuses on what I am doing, or practical ways to make something happen. All of us may use all of these different ways to influence – and indeed the most effective may be to include all three – reason, stirring of the emotions and a challenge to action.

After exploring these kinds of influence further I go on to suggest that the best kind of influence is by inviting – and giving the other person freedom to respond – or not. This may seem the antithesis of what we want to do, but in fact it is the most effective.

Influencing through reason

Influencing using the head entails knowledge, reasoning, rational thought, scientific method, articulation of ideas. In general, education, and tertiary education in particular, teaches us this way of influencing – and influences us in this same way. School debating teams are giving students practice in the art of rational persuasion, convincing argument, marshalling of facts. Often the person with the greatest knowledge base can win a debate, because for every argument of the opposition they can produce facts. The team also look for a fault in the reasoning of the other side, 'You said the majority want to pass this motion, but where is the evidence that this is what the majority want?' 'You have said that smoking causes lung cancer, but what is the research that proves this?'

The climate change debate has been a case in point. It has been difficult to amass evidence of climate change when there are such natural variations in climate patterns anyway. It is only as slow careful research, measuring levels of carbon dioxide, of oxidation in ice core samples, and temperature change in the ocean, amasses facts and finds patterns that more definite claims are now being made. Part of this process is known as 'scientific method.' High-school science classes teach the basic understanding of scientific method. The process begins with a specific hypothesis, 'Red cars speed more often.' A method is devised to measure speeding – for example certain stretches of highway and freeway are chosen – and argued to be representative of the city/state as a whole. Measurement devices are installed. *All* speeds of *all* cars are recorded for a set period – a period which is agreed on as covering 'typical' times. The results so gathered are analysed statistically. In comparing the average speed of red cars (and of course red must be defined), with cars of all other colours it may indeed be *proved* that red cars speed more often. It could then be argued that red cars cause their drivers to speed more often – but this of course is faulty logic. It is more likely that drivers who are more likely to speed are attracted to red cars. Further research would be needed to test that hypothesis: 'The colour red arouses the driver to speed,' or 'People who already have a record of speeding choose to drive red cars more often than other people.' So the scientific process continues, one piece of research building on the previous one.

People who have not learned to use this process, or the healthy scepticism it teaches, are more likely to be taken in by specious claims. For example, certain new products are often claimed to have almost miraculous effects. 'This herbal remedy cured my son's dyslexia.' Scientific method would demand that other possible causes be examined – did the teaching method change, were new glasses prescribed, was Johnny finally healthy enough, or getting enough sleep that he could concentrate properly? Anecdotal evidence is not accepted by the logic of scientific method. Maybe Johnny did improve because of the herbs – but maybe he is the one in a million whom they help.

Influence by reason necessitates careful logic, a good knowledge base, articulate presentation and an openness to persuasion on the part of the listener. Often the influencer's commitment to objective knowledge and 'presenting the facts' has the greatest impact. Presenting the facts and articulating the logic then allows the listener to 'make up their own mind'. We prefer to feel that we have the freedom to decide for ourselves.

Influencing through emotion

Often an argument is made more persuasive by the stirring of emotions. Martin Luther King's 'I have a dream' speech is influential because it paints a picture which is inspiring. William Wallace's speech in *Braveheart*, 'They may take our lives, but they'll never take our freedom,' provokes the listeners to courage and unity. If emotion is in itself a motivator, then arguments and preaching that appeal to our emotions influences effectively. How many of us are inspired or persuaded to do something, to live differently because we have seen a movie, read a book, heard a song? Identifying with another person's pain changes our perspective, gives us understanding of what it is like to be poor, to be addicted, to be Muslim, to be black – and helps us to be more compassionate to others. Feeling someone else's emotion – their anger at injustice, their terror in war, their desperation in a refugee camp – can change our perspectives on our nation's policies and exclusions.

Of course emotions can be misused as well. Some people are adept at manipulating through emotion – we feel guilty, sympathetic or ashamed, and so are persuaded to go along with what the other wants. Salespeople are taught to be aware of emotion and so to slant their sales pitch more effectively. Politicians and preachers often use emotional language to persuade us of their message. After the sales pitch or the political speech we may realize that we have been persuaded 'against our will' and wish to retract our decision. Or maybe we are influenced to feel superior and justified in destructive actions. How did Hitler influence the German nation except by somehow appealing to their desire to be superior – and rid of the implied threat of the Jewish people? Hitler's speech to his deputies in Berlin in May of 1941 in the second year of World War Two demonstrates this: 'I can assure you that I look into the future with perfect tranquillity and great confidence. The German Reich and its allies represent power, military, economic and, above all, in moral respects, which is superior to any possible coalition in the world.' The bringing together of morality and superiority is a trick to persuade the listener that what we do is justified. There is a similar implication in US President Bush's use of the term 'axis of evil' to justify war in his 2002 State of the Union address. Whatever our political position, we need to be aware of emotional persuasion, which may influence our decisions. Again, in the end, the most persuasive argument is the one that gives the listeners freedom to respond – rather than making them feel manipulated.

Influencing through action and command

A third way to influence others is through actions. We may consider speeches as just words and justifiably respond with an expectation that the speaker should 'Put their money where their mouth is,' act on their conviction. We may see through manipulation or emotionalism, but action is difficult to argue with. We are influenced most of all by people who 'have the courage of their convictions'. Men and women of outstanding influence – Gandhi, Mandela, Mother Teresa – are those who stand for what they believe, who act, and suffer imprisonment and hardship. These are the people who become our heroes, who we want to emulate. And in the arts, the heroes – Luke Skywalker, Harry Potter, Frodo Baggins – are fictional role models who act on their beliefs.

A further kind of influence, less relevant to friendship relationships but which also should be mentioned in the context of this discussion, is the imposition of power. This can be an enforcement of one person's will on another, 'You *will* do as I tell you.' The person with lesser power is neither persuaded nor manipulated – but simply commanded. In a more equal relationship this can be experienced as imposition of will – one person's will becomes dominant and the weaker person feels they have little choice but to go along with the other's decisions.

While each of these ways of influences can be effected constructively with positive outcomes, they can also be used to influence a person against their will, against their 'better judgement'.

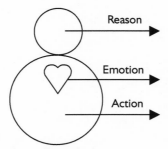

Influencing with head, heart and action

Try it

Think about a time when you have been persuaded, or manipulated, or even inspired to do something 'against your better judgment' – something which afterwards you wish you had not done. How did the influence happen? How did you come to go along with what the other person wanted? Were they offering you something in return, even something subtle like acceptance, belonging, a feeling of being courageous? Can you identify the 'method' they used – reason, emotions, action? If you were in that position again, how could you counter the influence? How could you clarify your boundaries?

Freedom, influence and boundaries

Influencing and being influenced relates to boundary keeping and respect of others' boundaries. Influence is about changing the other person, their action or ideas – often 'making them more like me' or what I would like to be. On what basis do we have the right to influence each other? Only on the basis of the other person's free choice.

If each of us is to be a free moral agent, making our own decisions and taking responsibility for those decisions, for our actions, then we need to act 'without undue influence'. To be a person of integrity and authenticity I choose my own actions, my own beliefs, my own way of living. And I give that freedom and responsibility to others also.

Learning what is me and what is not me, what is within my boundaries and what is outside them, helps me understand how influence works – from both sides. If I only have a fuzzy sense of my own boundaries I will easily be influenced by others' expectations, preferences, demands. Clarifying my own beliefs, attitudes and desires helps me to choose when I will be influenced by others and when I will not. If they offer me something which fits within my present sense of myself – or my aspirations and morals – then I can choose to accept their influence. If I do not want what they want for me then I can choose to set a boundary in place – and say No, this is not me.

If we carry this through, our relationship dynamics become very respectful of each other, upholding each other's freedom and responsibility. The most respectful I can be is to say to another person, 'This is my understanding, these are my feelings, and this is my choice of action. What is yours?' I am staying within in my boundaries, and giving them the choice to stay within theirs.

Presenting facts and reason can become persuasion. Using emotional language and provoking emotion in others can become manipulation – it is not the owning of my own feelings discussed in Chapter Three. Insisting on my way of doing things can become coercion, an imposing of my will. Stepping back from each of these allows the other person to choose their own responses.

A student in one of my classes brought this into sharp focus one day. We had been looking at these different ways of influencing others, and I had been trying to explain the freedom that comes into relationships when we let go the other person, choosing to state our knowledge, to own our own feelings and our own choices. The student interrupted with some agitation, 'How do I make people do what I want then?!'. And that is exactly the point. We give up 'making' people do what we want. We only invite response. We do not persuade or manipulate, cajole or threaten. This is how relationships work at their best.

Inviting response

Bringing together an understanding of how boundaries function and how we can 'influence but give freedom at the same time,' results in the following kinds of statements, in which the speaker owns their own reasoning, feelings, actions.

'It is my understanding that the work is completed except for one small project.'

'As I have read it, the research shows that using fossil fuels is one of the greatest contributors to greenhouse gas emissions.'

'If my reasoning is correct, Bill knew about this expenditure early last year.'

'I'm disappointed about this decision as it means I can no longer offer this class.'

'I'm angry that you have had to bear the brunt of these changes.'

'I am afraid that if this decision goes ahead, we will be unable to sustain production.'

'My preference is to finish the work today.'

'I have decided to take a break for the rest of the week, and come back fresh next week.'

'I am planning to focus on the initial project for the next two days, but then start the other work on Thursday whatever happens.'

Often, statements can contain aspects of reasoning, feeling and action:

'I am exhausted, and have decided to leave the new project until next week when I will be refreshed.'

'I've heard that we have a new worker staring next week so I have decided to leave this project so we can work through it together.'

'I'm really upset at the outcome, and need some time to work through our present options, before I make a decision.'

The main point is that we own our decisions, feelings and ideas, presenting them to the other person for their free response. Sometimes the statement of our position is all we need to say. At other times we may need to then ask for a response:

'I would prefer to let that go for now. Would that work for you?'

'I would really like to get this finished today, so I don't have the sense of it hanging over me. Would you be able to help me get it done?'

'I'm really upset that he's decided to leave. Can I debrief with you about it?'

'My understanding is that this product won't meet our needs. My preference is to change it. Are you ok if I go ahead on that?'

These statements have one or both of the first two aspects

followed by the invitation for response:

> Statement owning my feeling or knowledge
>
> Statement of decision, action, preference
>
> Invitation for response

Sometimes it is important to emphasize that the other person can make their own choice. 'I have decided to leave today, so that I arrive fresh for the celebration tomorrow. Do you want to come with me? Or would you rather come separately. What you do is up to you.'

We can own our own feelings but still give the other person space to make their own choice: 'I would be disappointed if you didn't come because I was hoping you would meet her. But it is your decision. – you know what else you have to do.'

Try it

Think of a conversation you have had in the last few days where you wanted to influence someone to your way of seeing things. How did you go about persuading them? Did you state your own reasoning, feeling, choices? Did you give them the freedom to respond?

Think now about how you might word your statements so they include your reasoning, emotions or preferences. How might you invite a response from the other person?

The most freeing kind of influence is invitation; a willingness to be open about my own reasons for choosing as I have, and then freedom for the other person to choose as they will. I have discovered that as I am willing to give other people freedom and to respect their boundaries, so I am living in a freer place of expecting them to respect mine. The freedom and invitation become reciprocal, experienced by all of those involved.

Leadership and invitation

Even leadership, at its best, is an invitation to follow – not an exercise of power. Historian Lord Acton (1834–1902) encapsulated warnings against power, 'Power tends to corrupt, and absolute power corrupts absolutely.' Invitation, a refusal to undue influence, gives liberty, and in Lord Acton's words, 'Liberty is the only object which benefits all alike.' Leadership which invites others to follow – invites the other to be influenced – is the mark of the best leader – according to Lao Tzu, the Chinese philosopher of the sixth century BCE: 'When the Master governs, the people are hardly aware that he exists... When his work is done, the people say, 'Amazing: we did it, all by ourselves!'[17]

This does not mean that we cannot be persuasive, that we cannot be emotional, that we cannot act on our convictions and hope that others will follow. The difference comes back, once again, to choosing to set my heart *towards* the other person, and to their freedom and maturity. A quote form Martin Luther King illustrates the use of emotional inspiration. In the 1960s turbulence of changes against racism, King, as an African-American, was dedicated to equality. He was not manipulating his 250,000 listeners. He was using emotional language to inspire them to persevere, to act with nobility and without bitterness, for the good of all Americans.

I have a dream that one day this nation will rise up and live out the true meaning of its creed: 'We hold these truths to be self-evident, that all men are created equal.' I have a dream that one day on the red hills of Georgia, the sons of former slaves and the sons of former slave owners will be able to sit down together at the table of brotherhood. I have a dream that one day even the state of Mississippi, a state sweltering with the heat of injustice, sweltering with the heat of oppression, will be transformed into an oasis of freedom and justice. I have a dream that my four little children will one day live in a nation where they will not be judged by the color of their skin but by the content of their character.

10
Constructive Conflict

After the honeymoon

Andrew and Patty had had a whirlwind romance. Having fallen madly in love and married as quickly as possible, they were now experiencing the reality that the honeymoon was over.

'We're just arguing all the time,' said Patty, close to tears.

Andrew nodded, adding, 'I don't understand it. We still love each other, we want to be together, but we just fight like cat and dog.' 'I'm so scared we'll split up,' Patty was really in tears now. 'But when I disagree with him, it's like this fire flares up in me, and I refuse to go along with what he wants.' Andrew nodded ruefully, obviously remembering a fight. Patty paused. 'It's as though I'm scared he'll leave me. But I'm even more scared he will force me to do what he wants.' She paused again. 'Not that he ever tries to force me – I just react so fast. And then his silence makes me mad so I pressure him to say what he wants!'.

Patty and Andrew were facing the reality of their individual conflict styles. In the first weeks of their romance they had been so in love that they had been willing to go along with what the other had wanted. Having married in such a short time, they had had little time to understand each other's underlying conflict style, or to experience the dynamics of the other's family.

As Patty began to look at her own reactions, she saw also some of the patterns of her family and how they had affected her. 'In my family my father held all the power. My mother did everything at home and he just expected that when he was there he would be waited on hand and foot. Everything was always what he wanted, whatever mum thought. I vowed I was never going to be like that.

And even though Andrew's not like my dad at all, it's as though when he disagrees with me it pushes a button and I react like he's going to be like my dad.'

Patty was caught by the patterns of her parents' relationship, and the very different patterns of her own – but still needed to work through how to resolve conflict in her own life. As she talked, she recognized that her parents had both had conflict styles – but different ones. Her father wanted his goals, no matter what the cost in relationships. 'And he's got that', said Patty with some anger at the realization. 'Well, he used to – he had everyone under his thumb, but now we've left none of us even want to visit. And although Mum has stayed he doesn't really even have a relationship with her.'

Patty's father wanted his own goals at whatever cost in relationships. Her mother never fought back. She sacrificed what she wanted to 'keep the peace', but ended up losing any real relationship as well. In the diagram below the conflict style that Patty's father used is the bottom right-hand one, 'goal at any cost', sometimes called the shark. Patty's mother had ended up with neither goals nor relationship (apart from the underlying goal of staying with her husband). Her style is the lower left-hand one – sometimes represented by the tortoise – a style of withdrawal.

As Patty realized the pattern she had grown up with – and vowed to leave behind – she realized one of the reasons she was so attracted to Andrew. It was because, in a lot of ways, he was the opposite of her Dad. 'He's really like a big warm teddy bear', she said, flashing him a smile. 'He goes along with a lot of what I want, but then when he disagrees, I get angry – and then if he goes silent on me I get angry again!'

'I guess my dad was the opposite of yours in a way.' Andrew was thinking out loud. 'He'd just go along with my Mum, and I've kind of copied him in that. Except sometimes I *do* say what I want, but then you get so mad at me. I guess we seemed to get on so well – we just did what the other one wanted because we so loved being together. Sometimes I do just want to give in to what you want. Maybe I'm just too selfish to do it all the time.'

He laughed.

'Yeah, and I do push you', Patty admitted. 'I think I'm scared I'll turn into my Dad and just push over you. I want to know what you want. That's not selfish – saying what you want! But then I don't want to go along with it! I guess I'm selfish too!'.

Andrew was realizing that his more frequent style of conflict was 'Relationship at any cost', the top left-hand corner, but when pushed he could fight too.

Different ways to approach conflict

Most of us can operate with more than one kind of conflict response – but nevertheless we will usually be able to pick the one we default to most often, or when we are under pressure. Commonly we copy our same-sex parent – or, as in Patty's case, vow not to, and end up doing the opposite. Our natural response will almost always be one of the three already noted.

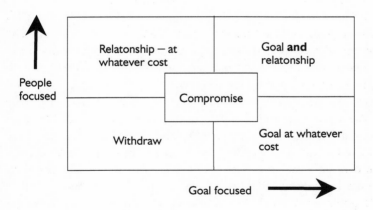

Styles of conflict response

Like Andrew and his father, the top left-hand quadrant is 'relationship at any cost.' Like Patty's mother, the bottom left-hand quadrant is 'withdraw' – and lose both goals and relationship.

Like Patty's father, the bottom right-hand corner is get the goal at whatever cost. Once we have recognized our natural default response, all of us can learn the 'Win-Win' interactions of how to move to a compromise or, better still, to achieve our goals and maintain the relationship as well, pictured in the top right corner.

Try it

Think back over any conflicts you have experienced in the last week or two – or potential conflicts. What was the conflict over? What did the other person want? What did you want? How did you behave? Did you withdraw, push for your goals, opt for relationship at cost of the goal?

Think of other conflicts in the past. Have you reacted in a similar way? Do you tend to react differently depending on the person the conflict is with, or the context?

Now think about childhood conflicts. Can you identify the conflict styles of your family?

Most of us need to learn how to practice the patterns of self-awareness and assertiveness needed for Win-Win interactions. Before exploring these it may be useful to review the boundary patterns and how they compare with conflict style. Usually our boundary patterns will be very similar to our conflict patterns. Andrew's choosing 'Relationship at whatever cost' is the mark of the compliant person – the person who can't say no, because they are saying 'yes' to a relationship. Patty's father was the bulldozer, the outright controller who resolved conflict by pushing for what he wanted, not hearing the 'no' of the other person. Patty's mother was probably an avoidant, not hearing the yes, giving up what she wanted and losing real relationship as well. The non-responsives – those who can't say yes – usually fit into the bottom left-hand corner too as they lose relationships because they do not respond to the needs of others. Of course, people being unique, we may be some other combination of possibilities – but the usual patterns are shown in the diagram opposite.

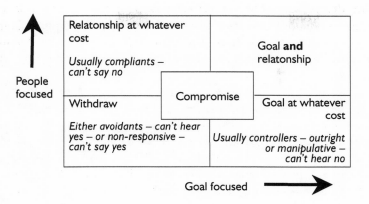

Styles of conflict response and boundary patterns

The diagram gives some clues to the needs each group tend to focus on, and the lies they need to discard, to be more effective in conflict resolution. Conflict resolution is often difficult – and we have to be convinced that it is worth the effort.

Try it

Identify your boundaries default pattern. (If necessary, revisit Chapter Two). Check whether your boundary pattern and conflict style line up with the diagram. If not, try to identify where you make the shift – that is, do different contexts or relationships bring about different styles? Do you have one usual boundary pattern, but conflict pushes some buttons, pushing you into a different 'personality' when you feel threatened? If possible, talk over your responses with your partner or a friend and check whether they see the patterns you are noticing.

Lies we believe

Many of us simply believe that 'conflict is bad and should be avoided', or we believe the lie implicit in the position we default to. It is an unusual family who has learned healthy patterns of conflict resolution, so most of us carry our unhealthy patterns and beliefs into our adult relationships, and like Patty and Andrew, only discover them when our love for each other pushes them out in the open.

Many of us have experienced hurtful or destructive conflict and therefore withdraw at the first inkling of disagreement, while others experience the adrenaline surge necessary to fight and defend ourselves. For both, the lie may well be that conflict is bad and the only responses are flight, fight or freeze. Others grew up in families where conflict was avoided or hidden, and so they also avoid conflict, feeling guilty about anger or argument.

Lie 1: Conflict is bad

The lies we believe relate to the default positions we choose. Andrew and Patty's conflict is exposing one of the lies – that 'it is selfish to say what I want'. Compliants, and those who choose the 'teddy-bear' position of relationship-at-any-cost, believe the lie that conflict will break relationship. Perhaps one of our parents said, or implied, 'Mummy/Daddy won't love you if you don't do what you're told.' Or perhaps we had brothers or sisters who only played with us when we did what they wanted. Or maybe we experienced a painful relationship break-up because we wouldn't go along with what our partner wanted. In any of these or similar experiences we suffer rejection as a result of choosing something the other person doesn't want. We 'know' that choosing what we want is at the cost of the relationship. We come to believe the lie that 'being myself' will cost me my relationship. What the compliant has to learn for adult life is that a 'relationship' in which I am not my 'self' is not a relationship anyway.

On the other hand, the Controllers, or those who insist on their own way, their own goals-at-any-cost, believe the lie that unless they do so they will somehow lose themselves. Their childhood scripts may have been formed by experiences where they had to fight to feel they were heard. Maybe their parents were busy or tired or preoccupied, or they were one of several children, and demanding what they wanted was rewarded by getting what they wanted. They discovered that 'God helps those who help themselves', and so learned to get on with it and help themselves, say what they wanted, as loudly as necessary until they got it. Or maybe they experienced humiliation when they didn't speak up, when they acted like 'a girl' or a 'wimp'. Or they learned that aggression is necessary in this world, or at least speaking up for what you want. Maybe they lost relationships anyway and so learned that you might as well get what you want, because love doesn't come for free. Or maybe they experienced a relationship with a person who dominated them leaving them feeling powerless, and vowed never to let that happen again. The lie they have to let go is, 'I have to fight for what I want or I won't get it.' The challenge is to trust that a real relationship will enable them to cooperate with another person and still achieve their goals.

Lie 2: I have to fight to get what I want

Sometimes this position is more subtle. We don't have to look like a shark to be one! Patty loved Andrew, and wanted to know what he wanted. Her vow to 'not be like her mother' caused her to fight for what she wanted, caused her ambivalence about Andrew expressing what he wanted. Others in this position look less aggressive than competitive. They may even be charming in their relationships – but they experience others' ideas and success as competition – it *feels* as though their needs will be overlooked if others look too good, or state their needs. So they are driven to compete, even to fight, however charmingly, because it feels as though that is their only way to be who they are, and get what they need. The lie is the same – unless I fight, unless I hold to what *I* want, I'll lose out.

The third group in the diagram are those who withdraw from conflict, letting go of goals and relationship in order to 'keep the peace'. The lie they believe is that they must 'Look after number one.' It may be worded more subtly. 'Be responsible', 'Don't expect others to look after you', 'If you want something done, do it yourself.' These statements become lies at the point where the person avoids conflict, avoids relationship, because they are not worth the pain. There is nothing wrong with being responsible; rather, the problem is withdrawal. Humans are social beings, and maturity demands relationships, including an ability to know and state my preferences. The avoidants and the non-responsives avoid either receiving or giving love, or both. Their childhood scripts fit with the pattern of looking after themselves. Perhaps as children they did not receive a lot of nurture, or only received love when they 'earned' it. Looking after themselves may be coupled, as with Patty's mother, with continuing to look after other people – but in the end not expecting a return. Or this person may be oblivious to others' needs, but quite self-focused around his or her own, even being a high achiever – but a loner, avoiding conflict by avoiding relationship. Whatever the subtleties, the lie this group believe is that conflict is not worth the cost.

Lie 3: Relationships are not worth the cost

The lies each group believes are linked to our understanding of self and selfishness. When Andrew wouldn't say what he wanted Patty would nag at him. She wasn't satisfied with him just going along with her – she was afraid she was becoming like her Dad – and she wanted real relationship too much to be satisfied with less. Andrew wants to be himself, wants to speak out his preferences, but then he wonders if he is being 'selfish'.

Being a self

Many of us – especially the compliants, those who withdraw into the left-hand side of the conflict diagram – are like Andrew. We think that if we go along with the other person we are being selfless, putting the other person first. The problem is that this may well be a destructive kind of 'self-less-ness.' When Andrew smiles and goes along with Patty, not telling her what he really wants, he is being self-less. The destructive side of this is that he may indeed be losing his 'self' – the real person he is. In this case being 'self-ish' may be the most constructive thing he can do – claiming the reality of who he is and what he really wants.

Some writers have called this destructive kind of self-less-ness 'de-selfing',[18] the letting go of a sense of who I am, who my 'self' is. In our society some groups particularly encourage this. Adolescent girls often go through a process of de-selfing, thinking that this is necessary to 'catch a man'. Some religious groups teach this process, believing it is right to 'put myself last', not realizing that in the process I can go over a line that makes me lose the reality of who I most truly sense myself to be.

Real relationships are between whole people – not two half people trying to find their completeness in someone else. I can only be a 'whole' person if I am willing to know the 'self' I am. The destructive part of all of this is being either self-centred or so de-selfed that I lose my self. In this sense of the word, being 'self-ish' is constructive. Patty's insistence on hearing Andrew's reality is important. Andrew's accepting that this kind of self-ishness is constructive for the relationship can take them forward into true intimacy.

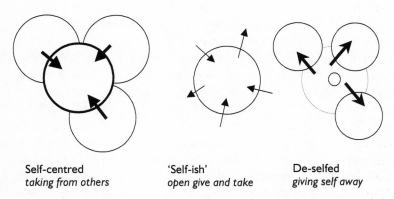

| Self-centred | 'Self-ish' | De-selfed |
| *taking from others* | *open give and take* | *giving self away* |

The diagram illustrates that there are different ways of being a 'self.' Self-centredness is an action of focusing only on myself, caring only what happens to me, and how outcomes of others' behaviour affect me. My self becomes intrusive on others, crossing their boundaries and demanding of them. In contrast to this a healthily 'self-ish' person is one who knows her/him-self. There is give and take across visible boundaries, and no intrusion in either direction. In contrast – but in the opposite direction – a de-selfed person is one who thought she was supposed to 'put herself last', and in giving her 'self' away shrinks to less than she really is. She allows others to cross her invisible boundaries and as a result loses touch with who she is and what she wants. A person who is 'most fully alive' is not de-selfed but knows who they are at their best. Some people have thought that 'dying to self' has meant we are supposed to de-self ourselves, whereas in fact it is the dying to *self-centredness* which brings life to relationships.

While this self-centredness/self-ishness/de-selfing process happens in the dynamic of all ongoing relationships, it is most clearly seen in the context of conflict. The self-centred person focuses on self and on his or her own goals, taking from others. The de-selfed person often does not even know her own goals, letting others have what they want in a relationship, and ending up with even less sense of self. Understanding what a healthy self is allows us to know what we want and to claim a two-way relationship of honesty leading to true intimacy. Andrew is moving back and forth between being self-ish and de-selfing. It is only as he recognizes the importance of truly being himself – and in *that* sense self-ish – that he can know himself, and invite Patty to know him. Patty, in contrast, has one parent who is aggressively self-centred and one who is deselfed – and she reacts to both of these patterns, trying to find her own way to self-hood. At this stage in their relationship there is huge potential for healthy self-development through honest self-disclosure and feedback.

I have used the word selfish in an unusual way. I am not trying to imply that all selfishness is good. I am highlighting another meaning of the word so that when those of us, like Andrew, fear we are being selfish, we can examine whether we are being self-centred or whether, in a healthy way, we are becoming more who we can most fully be. In this latter sense Andrew can understand self-ish as Andrew-ish – this is what Andrew wants, this is who Andrew is. And only then can he choose to *sometimes* put aside what he wants for the sake of Patty's needs, and the good of the relationship. And Patty can likewise be Patty-ish and be open about her needs – sometimes putting *her* preferences aside for the sake of Andrew's.

Conflict as necessary for relationship

Chapters Five and Six explored the steps necessary for intimacy. Scott Peck's second stage of community-making is chaos. This is the time of conflict. Many people, afraid of conflict, withdraw to pseudo-community. I have called this process of engaging in chaos the adversarial stage of relationships. I do not mean to imply that we pass through the adversarial stage and never return to it. Patty and Andrew have moved from the honeymoon of pseudo-community into chaos, into adversariality. If they are honest and open with each other, they will return to it over and over. It will keep their relationship alive. For some people this is very scary – conflict is necessary for intimacy, and indeed for a life-giving relationship. Honesty does not accept the half-life of 'keeping the peace'.

Why is conflict necessary? Because human beings are unique. I do not want my partner to be a clone or a mirror image of myself. It is inevitable that we will disagree. Maturity is finding the ways to disagree without destroying the relationship. If we simply withdraw to civility, to pseudo-community, we are opting out of intimate relationship anyway. While this might be appropriate in some relationships, or for a period of time, it should not be mistaken for intimacy, and the sharp challenge of honesty. Patty could simply leave Andrew alone, let him be 'nice' and agree with her, and avoid the conflict.

Using conflict to create stronger relationships involves several steps. First, one must recognize that conflict is a healthy part of relating and not something to be avoided. Most of us need to overcome childhood scripts to believe that conflict is good and to walk towards it with our eyes open. Second, we must recognize our present patterns of conflict – withdrawal, goal-oriented-at-the-cost-of-relationship, or relationship-centred-at-the-cost-of-self and one's own goals. Moving beyond this step usually takes an exposure of the lies we are believing. Third, we must begin the give and take of listening, and speaking assertively. Fourth, we must work towards a resolution.

Chapter Three explored owning our own feelings, Chapter Four, listening skills, and Chapter Seven included assertive communication. In a context of conflict all of these are much more difficult. In the heat – or hurt – of the moment most of us are more likely to accuse the other – to use 'You' statements instead of 'I' statements. It is much more difficult to listen to what you are saying when I am angry and want to say what is happening for me. It is much more difficult to speak assertively if my pattern in conflict is to withdraw, if something inside me is telling me I am risking the relationship if I say what I really want. Conflict brings out our inner scripts and so is an opportunity to get to know ourselves like few other events.

Holding on to myself

As Patty and Andrew come out the other side of their honeymoon period they have the opportunity to truly get to know each other. The challenge for Andrew (and for anyone who tends to favour relationship over goals, who tends towards not being able to say no), is to 'hold on to himself' in the face of conflict. Those of us who value relationships 'too highly', are too afraid of rejection and so we hide our boundaries, we defer to others, we let them have what they want – we let go our goals and needs.

'Holding on to myself' is knowing who I am and what I want – in the face of potential rejection. First, I have to believe that it is better to give my whole self, my real self to the relationship. Believing that, I need to hold on to that knowing, that awareness of self that I can identify at my best times.

As Andrew reflected on this, he commented, 'Usually I can think clearly and rationally. But I have noticed in the midst of an argument it feels as though my brain goes "fuzzy". As though Patty's arguments somehow cloud my brain so I don't know how to respond.' Our fear of being rejected, being hurt, can affect our ability to hold on to who we are. Somehow we need to slow ourselves down – even asking for 'time out' – so we can be true to what it is we want. Sometimes we may need the other person to repeat what they have said so we can listen again while still holding ourselves. David Schnarch, author of *Passionate Marriage*,[19] calls this 'self-soothing'. Most of us tend to rely on 'peace' (that is, non-conflict) in our relationships to help us feel good. When things go wrong between us and those important to us, we become anxious – whether we recognise our discomfort as anxiety or not. And we push for agreement again – in other words, we expect the relationship to soothe our anxiety. Self-soothing is the process by which I soothe myself, I calm myself, staying with the anxiety but not resorting to flight or fighting. This is surprisingly difficult for most of us, and so we don't even admit that it is happening. Staying with the anxiety of disagreement without giving in to the other person necessitates an ability to calm myself, to not give in to the animal instinct of running away.

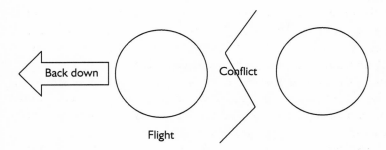

The person with the opposite instinct also needs to learn self-soothing. Those of us who fight also do so out of fear – fear of domination, fear of hurt. We have simply learned the opposite response to preserve ourselves. These are the people who claim their goals at the cost of relationship, who solve conflict by sticking with what they want. They particularly need to learn how to listen – without counter-argument or counter-attack.

Stepping out of the fight – staying with the conflict

This is the real test of listening skills – to listen while disagreeing with what the other person is saying. And here is a key to conflict resolution. If I can say what the other person wants then I am really listening – and showing them that I am listening. I can do this by starting a sentence with 'What you are saying is…' or, 'If I understand you correctly, you want…'. This kind of listening necessitates an ability to 'hold on to myself', to self-soothe. Pausing to show the other person I am listening to them takes a maturity on my part, a willingness to delay gratification long enough to show them I want to see their point of view.

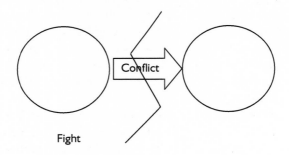

Fight

I remember a disagreement I had with a colleague, unfortunately one of those patterns where we both recognized the same old pattern of different points of view. I could feel my anger rising, and finally thumped my chair arm and said so. 'Jim, I'm getting angry here. Would you just tell me you hear what I'm saying!'. He held on to himself long enough to simply say, 'Yes I hear what you're saying.' It totally changed our interaction. I could feel my anger drain away, could even laugh as I said, 'Well, that makes all the difference!'

The problem is that we are usually caught in the heat – and fear – of the conflict. If one person can pause long enough to notice what is happening, they can defuse the tension, can choose to move themselves to the other person's position by listening and reflecting back to them what they are saying.

Usually, couples develop patterns of conflict – often one is aggressive and the other more passive. One person changing the dynamic can bring about an overall change – but it often feels very scary. It is the same movement as a shift from the Adversarial stage in a relationship to Acceptance – and it can feel as though we are going to lose something important. The more passive person can feel as though they may lose the relationship, the more aggressive person fears loss of power or freedom.

Often the most difficult part of this process is to stop the argument without stopping the disagreement, that is, to hold on to myself enough and what it is I want, what I disagree with, but to stop fighting. I can say something like, 'OK, let's try to understand what each of us wants. Can you say again what you want and I will try to put that in my words to make sure I understand. Then we can talk about what I want.' This is the moment when I need to remind myself I truly am *for* the other person. I really do want what is best for them. And I hold on to the reality that I want the best for myself also.

Using my listening skills at this point is essential; hearing what the other person has said and not exaggerating, minimizing or arguing, I say back to them what they want in similar words, truly trying to understand. Then when they agree I have understood (and I give them all the time they need to clarify and get it right), *then* I state assertively what it is I want. Clarifying what I want and asking them to listen and reflect back is important for this to be a truly reciprocal relationship.

Try it

Think of a conflict you have had. Try to articulate or write down what it is that you want. Then try and articulate what the other person wants. Which one is harder? Where is there a danger of 'losing yourself' or a sense of your goals? Or the other person's? If you are in a close relationship with a person you have had conflict with recently ask them to try out the process. Ask them if you can listen to them while they state what it is they want.

Reflect back to them what you have heard. Notice if you are able to keep your heart 'towards' them as you listen. Ask if you can get them to help you state what you want. See it as a joint project to understand each other.

Negotiation – getting what I want

Getting what I want begins with believing that conflict is constructive, an important step to achieving the goals of all involved. This involves letting go of the lies that I will lose either the relationship or my goals in the negotiation process. Then comes the hard work of listening and assertive speaking – while 'holding on to myself'. At this point I should be able to articulate what it is that I want, and I should also be able to state what the other person wants in words that they agree with.

The next step is trying to reach both our goals in a way that preserves the relationship. This is where honesty and self-awareness is essential. If I have a tendency to compliance I may well 'give in' too soon – but end up feeling resentful. In the first years of my marriage I believed that a good wife went along with what her husband wanted. I tried to practice self-giving love and forgiveness. Then, several years into our marriage, I discovered a mountain of resentment. I couldn't understand where it had come from. In fact it was the 'left-overs' of all the times I had given in without really knowing what I wanted. My husband hadn't understood that I had not agreed. The resentment was the indicator that I needed more self-awareness – more openness.

The first part of negotiation then, is to lay our preferences out on the table. It may even be possible to say, 'I really want this, and I would also quite like this, but that's negotiable.' The second part is to brainstorm ways to achieve both our goals. If we can learn to be creative and take the time we can sometimes achieve all that we both want. This is win-win. If I want to spend Saturday at the beach and you want to go to the city, it may be possible to go to the beach this Saturday and the city next Saturday. Or it may be possible to spend half a day in each place. Or it may be possible to split up and achieve what we both want – but separately. Maybe even invite other friends to accompany us if we want companionship. But if you *really* want the whole day for your shopping, or want me to come so we can buy something we both like, or it's urgent, then compromise may be necessary. Compromise is the recognition that neither of us achieve all that we want.

The 'compromise' square is in the middle of the conflict diagram above, indicating that partial goals are achieved and the relationship is at least maintained – but maybe compromised also. The top right hand square is the win-win position – the achievement of goals *and* positive maintenance of relationship, the process needed to find a solution which achieves good relationship and the goals of both parties is consensus. This is not the choice of the person at the top of the hierarchy, not the submission of one person to the other. It is an honest understanding of all the goals, and a discovery of ways to achieve these. It often takes longer than a hierarchical decision and it often takes more honesty and self-awareness than simply 'giving the other person what they want.' But in the end it develops strong trustworthy relationships.

Winning without losing

In his best-seller *The Seven Habits of Highly Effective People*,[20] Stephen Covey explores the idea of win-lose, win-win and 'win-win or no deal'. He clarifies the difference between compromise and win-win.

A commitment to win-win means that I refuse to 'win' without making sure that you win also – that is, we both get what we want. This is in contrast to the person who demands to get their goal even if the other person loses – this is a win-lose position. Again, it is in contrast to the person who sacrifices what they want in order to maintain the relationship. Losing what I want so that you win what you want is a lose-win result, in terms of the goal. The person who withdraws from the conflict *and* the relationship is in a lose-lose position – that is, both parties lose out.

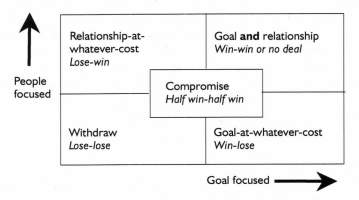

Styles of conflict response and achievement of win-win

The compromise position, as I have typified it, is half-win – that is, we both get part of what we want. The point Stephen Covey makes is that sometimes we should resist a compromise position. He suggests that it is tempting to compromise, to make a short cut to getting at least partly what we want. What he is advocating is that we stay with the consensus process – the more lengthy brainstorming and discussion that may be necessary to find a solution that gives us both *all* of what we want. He proposes that this is the 'real' win-win. He calls it 'win-win – or no deal' to emphasise that we should not 'make a deal' too soon – that we should hold out for a true win-win. This entails me truly listening to what the other person wants. And it means I must have my heart truly towards them, in order to be committed to the achievement of their goals as well as my own. This is a challenge for most of us in terms of our self-awareness, our ability to hold on to ourselves and our willingness to be honest – to value a relationship of two whole people.

Try it

Think of a conflict or recent discussion about goals. Did you get what you wanted? If so how did you get it? Did the other person get what they wanted? Did either of you have a commitment to win-win? Was there any practice of win-win or no deal? Can you think of examples of discussions where you have experienced win-lose or lose-win – or lose-lose?

As you reflect on the process, can you notice what you needed to do to achieve a win-win outcome? If so, is it possible to renegotiate a win-win outcome? Can you articulate what you could do differently in any future negotiation?

Traps and pitfalls

One of the most common traps in a conflict situation is to start fighting *against the person*, instead of fighting *for the goal*. Our past experience and present emotions combine to propel us to flight or fight. One of the ways we fight – destructively – is to attack the person. We might attack a weak spot, 'You just don't get things finished. You start but don't finish.' Or we exaggerate, 'You *always* say yes to everyone else', 'You *never* listen to me.' Or we bring up old hurts, 'You're just they same as you were five years ago. There you are again, giving in to your mother.'

These are all destructive patterns which sidetrack from the issue at hand. The natural reaction is defence – which may take the form of a counterattack. 'And you don't even get things started.' '*You never* say yes to *anyone*.' 'And you will never let me forget that, will you.' And so the hurt goes on, back and forth. Frequently the real issue gets lost and each person is left angry and hurt, the relationship in tatters.

An accusation which involves an 'always' or 'never' is bound to fail. The immediate defence is obvious – one counter-example proves the accuser wrong. A far stronger argument is to stay with the facts, and to own my own feelings.

Another pitfall is to tap into old hurts. We may have left things unsaid for some time, but in the midst of the disagreement out come our hurts and frustrations. 'You accuse me of not doing what we agreed, but you've been late to every meeting for the past month.' The injustice of an attack spoils our good intentions to stay silent, and out tumble the accusations and counter-accusations. As a result some of us refuse to fight, staying in withdrawal mode, or just being civilized.

Some principles for conflict then are:

Focus on the issue not the person
Stay with the present issue not past ones
Own your own feelings
Use 'I' statements
Avoid always, never
Refuse to counter-attack
Ask for time-out
Make a time to discuss an issue
Put yourself in the other person's shoes

Try it

Read through the list above again. Which ones of these do I most often use already? Which ones could I focus on more?
Think of a specific conflict. Which of these principles did I, or the other person, ignore? Is there someone I should make a time with to resolve a conflict? Are there some old issues that resurface for me? How can I let these go?

Taking offence, giving offence

Conflict has two sides. Someone has given offence, and someone has taken offence. Hopefully, as we become more sensitive to the needs and preferences of those around us, we will give offence less and less often. Frequently, the person who gives offence does so in ignorance. They may cross an unseen boundary, or be unaware of the other person's history, or simply not have listened to the other person. A 'sin of ignorance' is usually easier to forgive than an intentional one. Giving offence intentionally may come from an old hurt, a choice to hurt the other person before they hurt you, or a reaction to present attack.

Taking offence is actually more often under our own control than giving offence. While giving offence is often in ignorance, taking offence is more conscious. We have certain expectations and beliefs and often taking offence is the result of the other person not measuring up to these. Taking offence is therefore our responsibility. Sometimes we can recognise that our reaction in taking offence is actually within our own boundaries. We can then take responsibility for our own reaction, own our own feelings, and release the person from our imposed expectation.

When my marriage broke up a number of friends were offended. At first I wanted to explain what had happened to regain their approval. In the end I was able to recognize that they had taken offence because of their beliefs and expectations. I was responsible neither for their offence nor to fix it – it was within their boundaries. I had to live with the consequences in the relationship, but I did not need to carry the responsibility or the guilt for their reactions. In this sense, we need to develop a thick skin and learn not to take offence.

Sometimes, though, I may take offence and, try as I might, I cannot get past it. I need to own my own reaction, recognise it as my responsibility – but then go to the other person. This will probably take some of the internal work to be truly *for* the other person, as discussed in Chapter Seven. I am the one who has taken offence and I am now going to ask them to help me to let it go. In my experience the other person is often unaware that they have done something offensive. If we are truly on-side with each other we can both profit from this encounter. If it deteriorates into accusation and defence it is less likely to be constructive. If, on the other hand, I can explain what happened and own my reactions to it, there is hope for understanding and change from both sides. Often a relationship becomes closer as a result of being able to give and receive feedback in this way.

Try it

Think of a time when someone has been offended by something

you have done. Did you mean to give offence? If so was there a more constructive way you could have handled the situation?

If you did not mean to give offence, how did you feel when you found out? Did the other person tell you, or did a third person tell you? Were you able to discuss the issue? Was the outcome positive? If not, could you have done anything differently?

Now think of a situation where you have been offended, someone has done something at which you have taken offence. Did they mean to offend you? Did you talk to them about it? Did you talk to others? Did you own your own feelings? Was there a constructive outcome? Looking back, could you have done anything differently so the outcome was more positive?

Triangulation

When we are offended we frequently tell a third person about it. We are upset, hurt or angry and we want to vent our feelings – so we tell someone who is likely to see our point of view. This is a natural human interaction – and can be a constructive process. But it can also be destructive.

In my own life, I have discovered that the people who help me the most are those who listen and do not 'side' with me – but do come *alongside* me. When someone tells us of another person's offence against them it is tempting to side with them, to gossip, to agree about the other person's faults. While this may feel satisfying in the short-term it is not constructive to relationships on either side. On the other hand, it is often not very helpful to give advice if I am listening to someone venting. Often that is all they want to do – vent their hurt or anger. If I can listen, and be there for them, they are then more likely to be able to go on and find a positive way forward themselves when they are ready. When I tell a friend of my frustration or fury, I am most helped when they listen, hear my side of the story – and give me space to work out what to do next.

Triangulation is when a third party gets pulled into the conflict – a triangle is formed with the third party now a part of the problem.

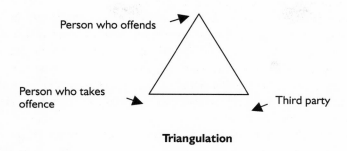

Triangulation

Triangulation happens when the third party takes up the offence of the offended person, or takes responsibility for trying to fix the problem. This becomes unhealthy for everyone involved. I cannot know all the history of the relationship, I cannot know what will bring healing between the two people. Sometimes the third person gets so drawn into the entanglement that the issue begins to be their issue, more than it ever was for the other two. This usually happens because the third party has unresolved issues of their own – and takes out their hurt or anger on to the present 'offender'.

This is a boundary issue. Other people's problems are not my problems. I can be a listening ear but if I try to solve or intervene I am on dangerous territory. I must be very careful if I am to 'take up my brother's offence'.

One of the most destructive relationship patterns demonstrating triangulation is in the children of divorced parents. One parent uses the children to send messages to their former partner. The children get entangled in conflict-at-arm's-length – and the children become the ball batted back and forth between the parents, both of whom they are trying to please. However tempting it is, the parents need to resist using the children in this way, and keep the issue in the boundaries it belongs in.

Those of us who are compulsive helpers or rescuers (or who have unresolved hurts) are the ones most likely to get drawn into triangulation. We need to learn to own our own feelings, and respect the boundaries of all of those involved. If we are to talk to someone about a third person one of the safest ways to do so is to be honest about who said what, what I think, what my perception is, and to step back and allow others to make their own decisions. If I pass on information I probably need to make it clear to both parties that that is what I have done – and again step out, and let their interaction continue.

Sometimes we need to adopt a 'no comment' approach, or plead 'conflict of interest', or even resist the temptation to 'hear the gossip'. When I am trustworthy in my relationships talking about a third person, others learn they can trust me in relationship with them also.

Try it

Think of a situation where you have been caught in triangulation. Were you the 'third party', the person offended, or offended against? How did you respond to the triangulation? Did you take on offence or responsibility that was not really your own?
What is your response when someone wants to vent their feelings about a situation with someone else? Do you get tempted to become the rescuer? Do you tend to give advice? What would you have to learn to do so as not to be triangulated in the future?

Mediation

Sometimes conflicts become so difficult or destructive that a third party is invited to help negotiate. This often happens when one person has more power than the other, so the person with less power needs an advocate, or at least someone to stand between them and the other party. Sometimes mediation is helpful when strong emotions are involved and one or both parties know they need help to hear the other person, or to articulate what they need to say. Many of us have experienced the 'loss of voice' that happens when we are confronted by a person who has more power than we do. It is not uncommon for the more powerful person to be unaware of the effect their power has.

As children, all of us experienced what it was to be in a position of less power. We learned to be 'seen and not heard', or 'not to argue with the teacher', or to 'just do it because I said so'. When we are in a position of conflict with a person higher up the hierarchy, or with power of reward, or expertise of some other kind, we can unconsciously revert to the childhood position of having no voice. Often a mediator can help defuse the power imbalance to give both parties equal voice, so both can feel heard. It is essential that the mediator does not take sides or become triangulated. Their role is to help the others hear each other – and then to step out of the interaction.

A formal mediation process often follows a set pattern. Initially, both parties may meet separately with the mediator, although this depends on the sharpness of the conflict, or the power imbalance, and is not always necessary. When the two parties come together, it is important, then, that both are heard. This is usually best accomplished by each person telling their story while the other listens. The task of the mediator at this point is to enable the one speaking to tell their story without interruption or intimidation. The mediator may use listening skills to help the person articulate what they want to say, or to continue with the story. When the first person has said all they need to from the past, the other person tells their story, again without interruption and with help, if necessary from the mediator. Both people tell the past story and also articulate what they hope for the future.

The point of the mediation is to find ways to achieve as much as possible of the future hopes of both parties. The aim is not to arrive at the same perception of past history. Hearing the other person's story may indeed help me understand the past differently. But it may not. The reality is that in a crime scene witnesses seldom perceive and remember the same details. In a situation of conflict our emotions are heightened and our perception is even more likely to be subjective. An expectation that mediation will bring about agreement concerning the past is an unrealistic goal. The best I can hope for is that at least I will be listened to. Knowing I have been heard is often very helpful in itself.

Once both parties have told their story to their satisfaction, and articulated their hopes for the future, the mediator helps them to discuss how they may achieve the goals each has expressed. If one person has been hurt by someone in some kind of professional practice it may be sufficient for the professional person to outline safeguards so that no-one else is hurt. Sometimes it may be enough for the person with more power to acknowledge their lack of awareness of their actions, and to undertake to try and act differently in the future. Occasionally some kind of public action may be agreed upon. Now and then one party will report back to a third party concerning changes they may make as a result of the mediation.

The point of mediation is to acknowledge the past, to accept different understanding of it, and to find a win–win, or at least compromise, solution for the future. Often a mediation process will facilitate an agreement to disagree, but with more care and consideration in the future. Occasionally there is reconciliation, with a meaningful relationship re-established.

Peacemaking

Many of us have recognized the destructiveness of war, the short-sightedness of international military conflict. We would count ourselves among those who want peace. But the actual process of peace-making in our own relationships is the real test of our attitude concerning conflict and terrorism.

How much am I able to listen to another person's needs or preferences? How much am I willing to compromise to give the other person what they want? How committed am I to the long slow, often tedious, process of consensual decision-making? How quickly do I revert to using whatever power I have to overrule and get what I want?

Learning to hold on to myself and stay with the process of conflict is one of the most maturing practices I can be part of. Truly working for a peaceful world involves the mundane – and very challenging – work of being self-aware and honest in my everyday relationships.

11

When Things Go Wrong

The hardest words to say

In the 1970s a romantic tragic book became a bestseller. The film version of *Love Story*[21] was advertised by huge billboards with this phrase; 'Love means never having to say you're sorry.' Romantic. Touching. But not true. Real love means learning to say you're sorry frequently and honestly.

The line from the movie was getting at the idea that when two people really love each other they will know their hearts are for each other and will be able to forgive without hearing an apology first because they will know the other is always *for* them. Few real-life relationships work like that. The reality is that we take offence, we get hurt, we make mistakes, we apologise, we forgive, we start again.

Most of us, when we were children, were made to say we were sorry. As a parent I tried to work out how to handle this. Was I to make my sons say they were sorry to each other – when I knew they weren't? Was it better to wait until they meant it? In the end I decided that a child has to learn the form – and then they can grow into the reality. I could see that when I have done something wrong part of the mending of it is to apologize to the other person. Knowing this only makes it slightly easier. 'I was wrong. I'm sorry', are still among the hardest words to say. There is something very humbling about admitting our mistake and asking forgiveness.

Part of the difficulty in saying the words is the profound meaning they have. To say 'I'm sorry', should really mean, 'If I could replay that action I wouldn't do it. I intend never to do it again.' Most of us are too caught in the emotion of the moment, in our own wants and perceptions, to really experience what the interaction was like for the other person, and to care enough to want to prevent a repeat performance.

I remember first realizing that in some cultures the words 'I'm sorry' had a different nuance. Several of us were washing and drying dishes together when one of the young women dropped a plate, breaking it. An older South African woman said, 'Oh Jenny, I'm sorry.' I was puzzled; I had seen the incident, I knew it had nothing to do with the older woman. 'But you didn't do anything', I said to her. 'No, but I'm sorry it happened', she explained. I rather like the South African kindness shown in her words, but in my culture saying sorry means I am admitting responsibility. And here is the rub. It is much easier to see what happened as the other person's fault. Saying I'm sorry admits it was mine, admits I am in the wrong, and I will try not to do it again. It is a vulnerable thing to do. It feels as though I am giving the other person power. In fact I am being honest to myself – but it makes me feel open to attack.

Apologizing well

Often we attempt an apology and do it badly. We might say 'I'm sorry if you were hurt.' 'Please forgive me if I did something wrong.' While this may be moving in the right direction, there is a problem with these apologies. The problem is that the speaker is not taking responsibility. Using the word 'if' spoils the message. What is communicated is 'I am not at fault.' A *real* apology has to contain several elements: responsibility, admission of fault, intention to change, request for forgiveness. 'I take responsibility. I am wrong. I will not do it again. Please forgive me.' Often these are difficult words to say – but they are necessary to clear the ground between us and allow trust to build again.

When I do not take responsibility, merely saying to you, 'Forgive me if you got hurt', the message is that it is *your* hurt, within *your* boundaries, and quite possibly *your* fault, but you should let me off the hook. It's the kind of apology we might have tried to get away with as children. As adults we need to look one another in the eye, and own our own actions and our intentions.

The apology that 'fits' the fault

Of course, because we are human, there are some people who will err in the opposite direction, saying sorry too often, apologizing for things that were not their responsibility, or which did not give offence. Usually these are people who are afraid of judgment or rejection so they say sorry too quickly. Either way the apology does not fit the crime, does not squarely own what is inside, and only what is inside, my boundaries of responsibility.

When people can admit fault and apologize clearly, accurately, and straightforwardly, the relationship is built on clear ground.

The request for forgiveness is also important. It is sometimes difficult for the 'offended' person to let go. We 'nurse the coals of our wrath to keep them warm'. We can sometimes feel very self-righteous when we have been wronged. We may not want to let that go. Some people hold on to their hurt or resentment for years, destroying any possibility of a real relationship in the process. When you ask for forgiveness and I give it, some kind of real exchange takes places. You have let me off the hook. I am free to get on with life. If you then still hold a grudge against me, that is your responsibility and you are the one who suffers. In requesting and granting forgiveness we are in effect saying, 'We choose to put this behind us. We choose to relate again.' The ground is cleared.

Forgiving and forgetting are not however, the same thing. The old maxim, to 'forgive and forget' does not mean we are to pretend nothing happened. If I hurt you, then apologize and you forgive me, you are not required to pretend that I did nothing. You have learned something about me. You can choose to be on side with me, but that does not mean you pretend nothing happened between us. In extreme situations a person may forgive but then remove themselves from harm's way. Most interactions are not extreme.

Most relationships can handle a lot of apology and forgiveness if both sides are genuine. The relationship can deepen because of the honesty and vulnerability involved in the relationship.

Why so difficult?

Why is it so difficult to say 'I'm sorry,' and 'I forgive you'? Because there is a significant interchange in these words. To say the words honestly requires a profound willingness to be humble, and vulnerable – to admit our humanity, and our need of each other.

There is a principle in these exchanges which carries over into other interactions; a willingness to take the position of humility, of proactively admitting that I am – or may be – the one at fault allows the other person to be more vulnerable also. This communication takes practice.

Patty and Andrew have been learning to be more open with each other, to process their disagreements while holding on to themselves. Then comes a crunch point. Patty's mother wants them to visit for Andrew's birthday. Patty doesn't want to go, she wants it to be a special day with just Andrew and her. But Andrew, wanting to please his new in-laws, feels obliged to go. 'There you go again', Patty says angrily, 'Not saying what *you* want!'. Andrew withdraws to watch the news. Patty, provoked yells at him, 'Well you go then, but I'm not going to!'. Andrew, now in a no-win position, says nothing. Patty storms off to do the shopping.

This has become a point of contention for Patty and Andrew, one of those places which could become a no-go zone for years to come. Schnarch calls these points 'emotional gridlock', points where we disagree but can't seem to find a way past the disagreement. Longer-term relationships often have these points, and unless they are dealt with, more and more of the relationship gets stuck in no-go zones. It feels too risky to venture into these areas. But Andrew and Patty have not been together too long. They are still flexible enough in their relationship to take the risks. But if they are to talk about the issue without escalating the argument, one of them will need to be vulnerable.

Frequently, but my no means always, men are higher risk-takers than women when it comes to physical activities – sports, adventures and so on. Often, though, the women are the risk-takers when it comes to relationships. This is true for Patty and Andrew, although Andrew is learning to be more open too. While out shopping, Patty meets a friend and lets off some steam. By the time she gets home she's less upset with Andrew. She has been carefully reflecting on the words she can use to get them back on side. Here is the point of vulnerability and, with it, a feeling of being at risk. This is Patty's chance to break through old patterns of self-protection. She thinks about what Andrew has said about his points of vulnerability too. She knows that above all he wants to feel loved.

She goes in and sits down with him, 'Andrew, I love you and I want you to have a special day for your birthday. I don't want to spoil it for you. Help me to understand what *you* would like.' Andrew is rather cautious. Is she going to react if he does say what he'd like? She goes a step further. 'Really. I'm going to try not to react. I'm sorry I said I wouldn't come if you went to my parents. I'm willing to consider it if that's what you really want.'

What Patty is doing here is choosing to be the vulnerable one. Admitting we might be wrong, saying sorry, stating the intention to be different, all take a surprising amount of courage. If Andrew refuses to respond he can help lock Patty into her old patterns. Being vulnerable in interactions is the best way to invite the other person to be vulnerable. But it's risky. The other person doesn't have to respond. This is the moment when they could get back at us, hurt us more. That's the risk. Andrew could ignore Patty's approach. He could use the moment to tell her that she is *always* trying to manipulate him to what she wants. He could damage the relationship for years to come by telling her that he hates her family and *only* goes to see them out of obligation. There are many ways to use a moment like this destructively. Or he could accept Patty's truce flag and try to work out a solution that would please both of them. Or go a step further and use the time to examine his own defences too. 'And I'm sorry I didn't answer you. I want to get better at knowing what I want and not feeling obligated. I just don't know what to say when I feel caught between people like that.'

Patty and Andrew may indeed help each other, more than anyone else can, to change their childhood scripts. But changing scripts feels dangerous, making these words the hardest ones to say.

Try it

Think of a point of conflict – either an actual interchange, or a pattern that you find recurring. How do you tend to defend yourself? What are the words or actions you use to provoke the other person?

Imagine what you could say to be on side with them. What is your point of vulnerability in this? Is their something you need to ask from the other person, to help you say what you need to?

Active peacemaking

As we learn to hold on to ourselves and practice being assertive and being vulnerable, these interactions become easier. This is the practice of active peacemaking mentioned in the last chapter. Peacemaking is most effectively achieved from a position of vulnerability – not one of power.

This is hard for us to believe, and even harder to act on. It is much easier to make conditions of peace, or act generously, when we are in a position of power. But acting from a position of vulnerability has a profound psychological advantage. It gives the other person much greater freedom to respond. It invites a change of behaviour patterns that is much more difficult otherwise. 'Turning the other cheek' allows the other person to lay down their sword also.

It is important here to understand what is really meant by the term, 'to turn the other cheek'. Those of us who have difficulty saying 'no' often *think* we are turning the other cheek, when really we are just once again giving in, choosing to be a doormat, letting the other person win, even if we lose. A person who, when slapped on one cheek, turns the other, because *they are afraid to do anything else*, or because they are obeying an ingrained script, is not freely inviting change. They are just perpetuating violence. It is when I am slapped on one cheek and I am free to hit back, but *choose not to*, choose instead to turn the other cheek, that I am saying in effect, 'We could fight about this. I could choose to hurt you. Instead I am inviting *you* to join me in finding a non-violent solution, at possible cost to myself.'

When Ghandi and his followers broke the British law by making their own salt from Indian salt pans, and then lay down in front of the horses and guns of the British soldiers, they were 'turning the other cheek'. They refused to be violent themselves, and invited the British to find a non-violent solution. In the end the laws changed, and India gained her independence. When Nelson Mandela chose not to find a legal way out of the charge brought against him, but instead, in order to change an unjust law, went to prison for 28 years, he was turning the other cheek. In the end, apartheid was abandoned.

In human relationships, choosing a position of vulnerability *in order to change the status quo* invites the other person to come on side. It is a demonstration of turning my heart towards the other person so they can turn their heart towards me. It is different from compliance, different from lose-win. It is saying win-win or no deal. It is the emptiness, or acceptance, that leads to intimacy.

Let's look again at Patty and Andrew's argument above. She has just accused him of not being able to say no *again*. She tells him he can go to her parents but she won't come. She's hurt him and he has withdrawn. How can *he* hold out the olive branch, 'turn the other cheek', invite *her* to change her patterns? What would it look like for him to take the position of vulnerability?

He could meet her at the door, offer to help put away the shopping. Hold on to himself and own his own feelings. 'I'm sorry I withdrew. I *do* want to please your parents. But Patty I care about what you want too. And I want to learn to listen to myself as well. Can you help me brainstorm what I really might like?' Andrew is being honest, but letting Patty see his vulnerability. He is not giving in to what she wants but he *is* choosing *for* the relationship.

Of course, each person has to find their own way through the minefields of their own weaknesses and those of the other person. We each have to find our own words, and ways of saying things – and at first, like the ski-slope of Chapter Four – it will feel awkward and uncomfortable. And it will threaten our ego, an ego that is used to defending itself.

Defences

Sigmund Freud was the father of psychoanalysis. Although some of what he believed has now been generally discarded, his proposals about defence mechanisms have become part of everyday language and understanding. 'You're in denial', 'You're rationalizing', 'You're projecting', are perceptions that are informed by Freud's work. He believed that all of us resist change, resist exposure. We defend ourselves from the truth. We learn patterns of behaviour that generally get us what we want, and then we resist change, and defend ourselves from others trying to change us. Andrew's compliance is a defence mechanism to get what he wants – the acceptance and love of other people. Probably it worked in his family and through school. Its limitations as a total strategy are now being exposed, and he is defending himself from that reality. In contrast, Patty learned to fight for what she wanted. As part of that strategy she learned to look at what was at fault in the other person, to see any relationship breakdown as the other person's fault. And she, too, automatically defends herself from the reality of her own faults.

Denial is a commonly understood defence mechanism – a simple refusal to look at the truth of what is happening. Everyone else may be able to see that Tony is an alcoholic, but he is in denial. 'I can stop when ever I want to', he says. 'I just don't want to.'

Rationalizing is a rather more subtle process. We find some rational reason for why we have to keep behaving the way we are. 'I have to keep working sixty hours a week, because otherwise I can't afford the mortgage.' 'If I don't point out all my boss's faults, no-one else will, and he will never change.' We frequently convince ourselves that we are doing something for the best of reasons, when there is a much more compelling reason hidden below the surface – such as fear of change, unwillingness to let go of a role, fear of loss or domination.

Projection is a still more subtle defence. It is the process whereby we 'project' our own intention, fear or desire on to someone else, fooling ourselves that they are the one with the problem not us. 'I'm going to continue living with my mother, because she would be so lonely if I left', may well cover a fear of loneliness on the speaker's part more than the mother. 'Johnny would be so upset if we didn't go and watch his football game', may well say more about the father not wanting to let go of his son, rather then the son caring if his father is there or not. Patty's anger at Andrew's willingness to go to her parents may be more about her guilt at not wanting to go, rather than about his compliance.

Projection makes it doubly hard to look at ourselves. We are refusing to look at our own feelings, and we are choosing to find the fault in someone else. A willingness to look at our defences takes courage. A key may be that we are defending something that is valuable to us. Identifying what is valuable may give us clues to better ways to preserve them. Patty's unwillingness to go to her parents reflects her refusal to be dominated by her father, to be a doormat like her mother, and to protect Andrew from those patterns as well.

Try it

It is difficult to look at our own defences – because we put defences in place to protect us! Defences are indicated by the things we forget to do, by dreams, by overreacting emotionally, by hating someone irrationally – or falling in love with someone else. Disproportionate emotions are a good indicator.

What is something I continually 'forget' to do? What themes recur in my dreams? Especially repeating dreams? What are the qualities in people that I find particularly difficult to handle – can I see those qualities in myself? What qualities do I especially admire, fall in love with, put on a pedestal?

Ask a trusted friend to help you notice your defences. When you have identified a defence, try and articulate what value you may be defending.

Defending vulnerability

Our defences are designed to hide those things that we are anxious about. We keep ourselves safe by not looking too closely. We try to keep other people from noticing also. Our usual reaction to other people's defences is to back off. We interpret the No Trespassing sign and let them keep their defences – and illusions. Or we may attack them, causing them to dig their toes in even more. Defences act like a moat and castle wall, like a buffer between us and the other person, a Keep Out sign that shows our boundaries without a conscious or clear communication.

The difference between boundaries and defences is that boundaries are conscious, and boundary lines can be stated with straightforward clarity. Harry tells Tom, 'I'd rather not come to the soccer tonight as I have to work early tomorrow.' Defences are unconscious and therefore their communication is fuzzy and not open to discussion.

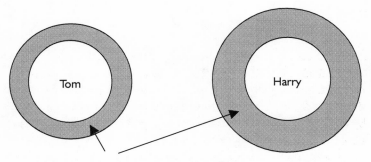

Defences – a buffer of protection

If Harry is telling Tom the truth then this is a clear boundary line. If, however, Harry is lying, bluffing or hiding things it is more likely a defence. For example, maybe Harry makes the statement above, 'I have to work early tomorrow' – except Tom knows he *isn't* going to work tomorrow. Or maybe Harry says that his partner doesn't want him to come – but Tom has just had a conversation with Harry's partner and she said she would like to come too. Or maybe Harry accuses Tom of never really wanting Harry's company. Any of these send a mixed message which basically says, 'Back Off.' Defences protect us from having to face the truth about ourselves.

Boundary	Defence
Clear	Fuzzy
Real reason	False reason
Self aware	Not aware
Invitation to negotiate	No invitation
Underlying message: We can talk	Underlying message: Back off

While boundaries create clear communication – and therefore an invitation to further discussion – defences tend to close down discussion as the hearer is left with the 'Back Off' message and lack of clarity about the real issues. If Harry says simply, 'I have to work early tomorrow' and that's the truth, then Tom can suggest that he can help with what needs to be done. If Tom knows it's not true, or is accused of not really wanting Harry's company, he is left with nowhere to go for further negotiation.

Finding the best distance

In team sports we each have a role or territory. The centre forward stays near the centre of the field while the wing runs along the sides of the field. As team members get to know each other, they learn each other's idiosyncratic style and know how much space to give each other. Tom might like the wing position but may stray across further to the centre when he sees an opportunity to grab the ball and run with it. If he does this successfully, other team members learn to give him the space.

Each relationship has to find its own space and distance in order to be most effective. Sometimes we move in too close – and then have to back off. Maybe Harry has been feeling pressured by Tom and wants their relationship to be a bit more distant, so he is sending (quite possibly unconsciously) some 'Back Off' messages. Tom will probably take the hint.

Most relationships have this dynamic quality of moving in and out until a comfortable distance is found. It is difficult to back-track when a relationship is close and then becomes more distant. Usually we move closer slowly, checking the other person and our own comfort levels. And when we are not comfortable we back off, give hints, or send unconscious 'No Trespassing' messages.

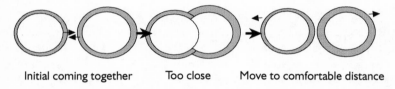

Initial coming together   Too close   Move to comfortable distance

Finding a comfortable distance in relationships

Both people have to be in agreement in order to find the comfortable distance for a relationship to function. Work relationships and specified roles often define positions and practices for us. Friendship and casual relationships are more open-ended. Family relationships, once the family has grown up, can also have a great breadth of possible roles and distances. Often the person with lower needs for the relationship will dictate the distance that is comfortable for them simply by not being available or not responding. Usually, then, the distance at which a relationship functions will settle without specific discussion – because discussion *about* the relationship is often awkward. In some relationships the coming closer and moving away continues depending what is happening for either of the people involved.

Many relationships will have this dynamic quality, like a dance step where each partner moves in and out. Giving the other person space lets them choose to move in closer again.

Try it

Think of a number of different relationships, especially with people you have met recently. Can you identify the drawing together, pulling away dynamic? Who pulled away? Who tended to go closer?
Are there some acquaintances or friends with whom you would welcome a closer relationship? Are there some relationships where you would prefer more distance? What have you done to indicate your preference? What might you do?

Some people send 'Back Off' messages without realizing that they are doing it. Remember the gut-people in Chapter Eight, those who have an against-energy? Their natural way of being is an 'against' one, and they don't always know they are sending these messages. A man I know, Trevor, is like this. He has a very kind heart, but the initial impression he often gives comes from the against-energy. He gets stopped by customs officials and held up in immigration checks. He doesn't mean to do it, but when he is on the defensive they pick up the against-energy and are suspicious of him. Some of our friends might be like that, sending 'Back Off' messages they are not aware of – and consequently, they are misinterpreted.

Moving through the defence – challenging the buffer
In the scenario above Harry is sending some 'Back Off' messages. He usually finds that people keep their distance when he does that and give him space to work out his own issues. Tom and Harry though, have been friends for years, went through school together, know each other's families, are good mates. And Tom knows that when Harry starts withdrawing like this it means that he's really

struggling with something – his work, his marriage, his alcoholic father. And he knows too, that Harry always finds it difficult to ask for help, not even realizing he's withdrawing until he's cut everyone off. So Tom walks into the No Trespassing zone.

This is one of the hardest things to do in relationships because we've experienced the 'Back Off' messages before – in this or other relationships. Most of us do not invite conflict. We've been socialized to know that when your friend doesn't want to see you, doesn't want to talk about it, you give him space. But Tom knows his friend, and cares about him and his family, and can therefore take some risks. He walks into the no-go zone.

Most of us have little experience in this, and we find it awkward. The most important consideration to get to first base is, 'Is my heart for my friend? Am I in a side-by-side position here? Have I let go of judgments?' Or am I really just 'coming out of frustration', wanting to give him a 'piece of my mind'?

Having checked my attitudes, and having done the internal work necessary to be side-by-side with my friend, I can walk into the buffer, the no-go area. This usually involves self-disclosure (with 'I' statements) or feedback, or both, and is usually best done in a safe place, and tentatively. 'I've been noticing you've been withdrawing lately....'; 'It seems as though you're not wanting to spend time with people...'; 'I feel rebuffed by you lately. I'm wondering if it's just my interpretation or if something is happening with you?'

Whatever Tom says, it will probably feel awkward, as he knows he is in a No Trespassing zone already. He may need to give a lot of assurance, as Harry is probably feeling over-sensitive as it is. He could try to ask permission to talk about the sensitive areas, he may even have to back off if Harry refuses entry. It might be worth leaving the door open for another try later, 'Well, I'll check you again in a few days.'

Talking about what's happening in a relationship is awkward for most of us. You may want to revisit Chapter Eight. The main point here is that we are stepping outside the usual give-and-take of the relationship and commenting on the process from an on-looker's position. Most of us do not have a lot of practice in this. Tom is probably going to have to take some risks and make himself vulnerable to help Harry come out from behind his wall. That's why self-disclosure is often a helpful way to go at this point. Tom might even share some of his own pain to help Harry know he's not going to attack him, or try to advise, fix, heal or convert. 'When I saw you looking tired today it reminded me of how I felt when my mother was dying of cancer. The awful feeling I had that some foundation of my life was crumbling.'

Try it

Think of a time when you have felt embattled, have pulled up the draw-bridge and retreated behind the castle walls. Did anyone try to talk to you? What was that like for you? How did you respond?

How could anyone have helped you? How would you have preferred for them to approach you? What might they have said or done to help you let down the draw-bridge?

Is there anyone who may be needing you to approach their No-go zone?

Marriage break-ups and death seem to bring out everyone's philosophy of life. Threatening situations make us want to fix, heal and convert even more than usual. Trespassing in a no-go zone therefore needs careful evaluation – am I doing this for the other person? – or to make *me* feel better?

Backing out of a relationship

Walking into someone else's no-go zone takes courage to overcome the awkwardness. 'Changing the rules' of a relationship is almost always uncomfortable. Changing the rules in the opposite direction – that is, deciding to have a more distant relationship – is also very challenging. It is very difficult to no longer be partners, to move from friendship to being acquaintances, to distance a once close relationship. One or both parties will feel rejection, and react accordingly.

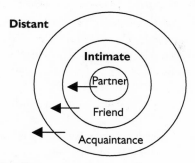

Backing Out

John and Alice have been seeing each other for a year, but now Alice is starting university and John is beginning a new job. Alice senses that their common ground is becoming less and less and she wants to be free to meet others more similar to where she is at, but she doesn't know how to tell John in a way that won't hurt him.

David and Bruce have been casual friends, but now David has got a teaching position at Bruce's school. Bruce senses that their new roles in the same workplace will change how they relate. He is not comfortable with meeting David socially any more. He doesn't know how to explain this discomfort.

Sandy was going through a crisis when her daughter was in a psychiatric hospital. Her friends Tim and Sue tried to help by letting her drop in any time. The crisis has now passed, but Sandy still drops in at all hours. Tim and Sue are wondering how to tell her that they would like her to change this, without her feeling they are rejecting her.

Most of us try to avoid talking about our preference to 'back out'. We tend to just not return calls, not 'see' the other person – hoping they will take the hint. They might – but still be hurt – and wonder what they did wrong. It is much 'cleaner' to talk about the change.

If the change has been brought about by some negative event – John was coming on too strong sexually, Bruce and David's wives had an argument, Sandy came and invited herself to a barbecue when other friends were there — then it is much harder for the other person to keep a 'side-by-side' attitude. Being as objective as possible is the most likely starting place for positive future interactions. And the same principles apply — taking responsibility for the change, using 'I' statements, not accusing, reassuring the other person as much as possible, but making as clear a boundary as can be made. 'I'm sorry John. I need some space. I didn't know I would feel like this, starting uni, but I just want to start fresh by myself. Maybe we can be friends later, but right now, I'd rather not see each other.'

'David, I'm not sure how it's going to work out with you at the school. Can we just play it cool for a while — see how it is for us to relate as colleagues before we see each other socially this semester.'

'Sandy we really wanted to be a support to you when Sharon was not well. We knew you were going through a really tough time, and we're so glad to see how well you've done. Things have changed a bit at home and we want a bit more time alone now. Would you be able to ring before you drop in to give us a bit of a warning so we can let you know if it's convenient or not?'

Any of these could cause offence, could mean the end of the relationship. Relationship change is risky and feels threatening. People often interpret change as rejection and their history increases the emotion of it. The aim is to find a win-win outcome in a potentially destructive situation.

Try it

Do you know someone whom you have been avoiding? Is there a relationship which you would rather was not as close as it has been? Or where you have been receiving mixed messages from someone else? Can you think of a win-win way to address the changes in the relationship? In what way would being clear about your preferences and boundaries affect this relationship? What are the risks? What positive comments can you make to help you and the other person move forward?

Backing out of sexual relationships

The next chapter explores romantic and sexual relationships, recognizing how the heat is turned up in these relationships. Everything is intensified, including need, desire, rejection and loss. Our history of relationships impacts powerfully on our romantic and sexual relationships, expectations are charged with former emotions, actions and words become permeated with other meanings.

In our sexual relationships in particular, we tend to 'pick up where we left off' with the last one. Our first romantic partner often carries special significance and each step to closer sexual intimacy is significant. Next time around, we are often less aware of the steps and we move quickly into a closer stage. With each relationship the 'sexual fuse' gets shorter. Whereas a teenage girl may have decided she would never kiss on a first date, she may find that after some years and numbers of relationships this has changed to no intercourse on the first date. The sexual fuse gets shorter, she moves through the sexual intimacy stages more quickly.

There is a similar but opposite dynamic in backing out of sexual or romantic relationships. It is as though the 'fuse' has been burnt and we do not know how to relate at an increased distance. Either the spark of desire is still too present, or the hurt of rejection is too near, for one or other of the former partners.

Alice, just starting university, is probably right in expecting that she and John are better not to see each other for a time. Juggling their old feelings along with different preferences and new experiences is extremely difficult. All relationships are prone to misunderstandings, romantic ones and 'in-the-process-of-distancing' ones especially. An affectionate friendly smile from Alice might be taken as a come-on by John. A casual hi-and-bye in the shopping centre might be taken as an intentional brush-off. It is as though they both need to grow a new buffer zone between them. Boundaries need to be extra clear and solid to withstand the change. Each partner needs to withdraw and reinforce the foundation points of relationship bridges before traffic can recommence. The boundaries themselves will probably need redefining – a difficult process when each person is trying to understand how the relationship now works.

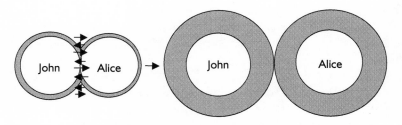

Changing the buffer zone – giving each other space

Former marriage partners in particular have great difficulty in changing their relationship. Rejection by one or other partner is too painful. There is usually hurt and disappointment on both sides and it is difficult not to blame the other person. It seems that at the beginning of a relationship, when we are at the civilized level of relating, we have certain inherent rules of relationship – to be polite, to show basic courtesies. Yet once partners have been close and are now moving further away, one or other of them may think all the rules can be broken; as though now a war has been declared and they can toss hand grenades, or set dynamite under the bridge struts. This is very destructive, especially when children are involved. We need to choose to obey the same social rules we would for someone we hardly know, choose to keep our hearts towards the person we were once close to. Sexual and romantic relationships magnify the power of the experience of love – and the experience of rejection – in the relationship.

12
Sex and Romance

Sexual energy

Was this the first chapter you turned to? If so, you are like a great proportion of humankind – experiencing sex and/or romance as a major motivating factor, a source of energy – and often enough, pain. Turning to this chapter out of order illustrates one of the major points I want to make by including it – that sex and romance amplify almost all the feelings, experiences and principles discussed in earlier chapters.

The delay of sexual relationships and romantic longings until puberty should give each child time to work out the basics of relationships in a loving, accepting context – without the complications, the agony and the ecstasy, of sex and romance. Even so, most of us are not ready for the flood of emotion, the flood of physical desire that we experience in our teenage years.

The fact that children take so long to reach maturity means they need parents, caregivers, grandparents – yes, at best a whole village – to raise them for a decade or two. Sexual relationships work best when they are in the context of long-term relationships – which could then stay cemented long enough to raise children.

The sexual freedom that some of us experienced after the invention of the contraceptive pill and before we knew about AIDS made us think we could enjoy sexual encounters without long-term commitment, that sex was to be enjoyed for its own sake, and without strings attached. Some of us would like to continue with the illusion. But my experience at least, is that it doesn't work. When I was at university in the seventies I experimented, like most of my peers. And I watched what happened to myself and others as a result. One of my deepest learnings was that a good sexual encounter was like a powerful adhesive, gluing two people together in a way that could only be reversed by tearing at least one of them apart. It is as though we build a concrete bridge in the space of an hour – with all cables attached and moorings in place. Except that if we then pull away, the cables pull out the chunks of rock they are attached to, and the moorings drag out parts of the river bed. Of course I am writing as a woman, and as an individual, I cannot say if this is what it is like for everyone – but it is certainly the risk.

When I was married and in a long-term, committed, faithful relationship for quarter of a century, I experienced the way sex helps strengthen the bridge of our relationship over and over. The ecstasy, the fun, the playfulness, all help to heal and comfort, enhance and bring reconnection. The delight in giving the other person pleasure and the luxury and excitement of receiving such pleasure from another creates a bond as little else does, and in fact can challenge us as other relationships can seldom do.

Sex and commitment

Robert Sternberg' book, *The Triangle of Love: Intimacy, Passion, Commitment*,[22] sets a context to relate different aspects of relationship. This context then helps a sexual relationship to work most effectively. The triangle of love shows these three kinds of love and how their combinations form different kinds of relationships. Sternberg suggests that all three present together create the strongest kind of love – consummate love.

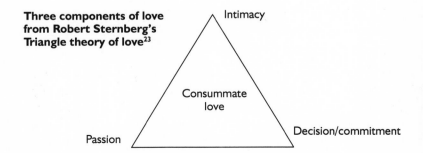

Three components of love from Robert Sternberg's Triangle theory of love[23]

Intimacy

Consummate love

Passion

Decision/commitment

Sternberg describes intimacy as involving closeness, bondedness and warmth – liking in the fullest sense of the word. Passion means romance, physical attraction, sexual consummation. The third component has two aspects, one short-term and one long-term. Decision is the short-term aspect – deciding that you love someone, commitment, is the long-term maintenance of that love.

As shown in the diagram, when all three components – passion, intimacy and commitment – are present, this produces consummate love. But other combinations are possible. Intimacy and passion are romantic love, intimacy and commitment form companionate love, and passion along with commitment (but without intimacy) is fatuous love. Sternberg also names the possibilities of just one kind of love being liking (intimacy alone), infatuation (passion alone), empty love (commitment alone). While Sternberg points out that these are extremes, they nevertheless give us some handles to think about our own relationships.

Try it

Think about some past and present relationships. Which of Sternberg's components were/are present? As you think about each relationship, would you say that it fits the name Sternberg has given it? How would the relationship change if another component was added?

If you have a partner, are all three components strongly present? Does one component need some nurturing? Can you talk to your partner about their perceptions around these ideas?

Sex and intimacy

More recently Sternberg has written a book called *Love is a Story: A New Theory of Relationships*.[24] He is referring to the idea, currently rising in a number of contexts, that humans think more in terms of stories than propositions or concepts. We each hold stories or metaphors, images of how we think love should be – or how our lives should be. These may be unconscious, or at least unexamined, but they will influence our decisions and our expectations. Obviously if a couple have very different stories their actions and decisions around their relationship will differ, and may cause grief if they cannot discover the differences in hopes, expectations and dreams.

Sternberg's triangle gives some understanding as to how sexual relationships will differ according to whether the other components of the love triangle are present. His theory helps explain how intimacy and decision/commitment give a stronger framework for a sexual relationship to draw partners together, like the bridge mentioned in Chapter Seven.

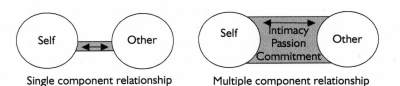

Single component relationship   Multiple component relationship

What happens to relationships that have only one component? Is it possible to have a 'relationship' which is only passion, only intimacy, only commitment? It does seem that we can have real friendships consisting of the intimacy component alone. These are not sexual relationships and frequently they would be between two people of the same sex. Some of the ancients believed that friendship was the deepest relationship possible. Many of the principles in this book apply to friendship relationships. Indeed a strong bridge of relationship can be built in this way. This chapter, though, is exploring the component of passion – sexual and romantic aspects of relationships, and how they contribute (and complicate), making the relationship work.

A relationship consisting only of commitment is termed empty love. Sternberg questions how it can survive. He suggests that maybe it is a relationship holding by a mere thread, perhaps because of religious sanction against divorce. He also questions the possibility of a 'relationship' that is only passion – suggesting that an encounter with a prostitute might fit into this category. Unlike intimacy, passion does not survive on its own. Sex and romance are explosive energy systems for forging relationships but need the reinforcement of other interactions to create a lasting healthy relationship.

The sexual crucible

Sex therapist David Schnarch tells us that a sexual relationship is a window into the whole relationship. Sex focuses on the dynamic of a relationship like a powerful spotlight. Every relationship involves give and take, meeting your needs, having mine met, sharing my preferences, clarifying my boundaries. A sexual relationship heightens these. The relationship works best when there truly is give and take, a meeting of each other's needs, an expression of preferences and a clarifying of boundaries; being able to be naked and accepted, safe in each other's love and commitment. David Schnarch proposes a 'sexual crucible'[25] – two counter-flows of energy: one towards growth, individuation, differentiation, and therefore confrontation of the other person; and one towards comfort and safety, and therefore avoidance and detachment. The outer circle of growth is anxiety producing – and may lead to termination of the relationship by growing away from the other person.

The growth cycle is part of the ongoing dynamic of a healthy interactive relationship. One person may be unhappy about some aspect of the relationship – disliking something the other person does, wanting more sex, looking for change of some sort. This recognition leads to an increase in anxiety. In a healthy relationship the partner wanting change needs to confront the other. This takes courage – and self-soothing is necessary.

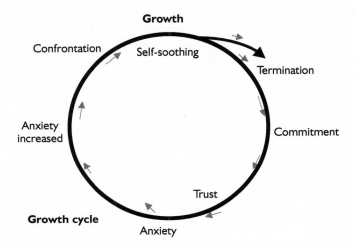

Growth

Confrontation   Self-soothing

Termination

Anxiety
increased   Commitment

Trust

Growth cycle

Anxiety

I need to hold on to myself, my own sense of what I want, in order to break any emotional gridlock and raise the matter with my partner. If all goes well the relationship is strengthened, commitment is increased, each of us knows we can trust the other more. If my partner cannot respond to my challenge, or I cannot accept their response – or lack of it – there is a danger of termination, a danger that my own growth, my own integrity will lead me out of the relationship. If termination is not an option, both partners are caught in a cycle of compromise, of shutting down in some way, to keep the partnership at whatever cost. If this route is taken, the inner circle is activated.

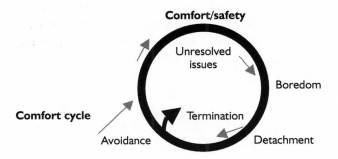

Comfort/safety

Unresolved
issues

Boredom

Comfort cycle   Termination

Avoidance   Detachment

The inner circle is one of safety and comfort. It is also part of the ongoing dynamic – and helps to keep the partners and the relationship safe. But without the outer circle it becomes stagnating and even suffocating. The inner circle is anxiety-reducing but does so by avoiding honesty. It results in detachment and unresolved issues – and could lead to termination of the relationship by withdrawal into oneself. We may not immediately think of this result as 'termination', because we are still 'in' the relationship – but it is really a façade, a pretence of relationship without the life – like Sternberg's empty love, it is commitment without passion or intimacy.

The two cycles work together. One or other partner may choose to opt out of the growth cycle and, avoiding the challenges of confrontation, moves into the inner circle – the comfort cycle. Anxiety is reduced and the status quo continues.

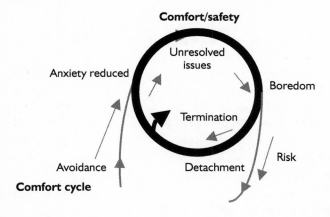

Peace is restored for a time, but then one or other partner becomes bored, or notices a sense of detachment and wants greater engagement. This partner takes a risk and moves back out into the growth cycle – with an increased anxiety as a result.

Sexual relationships as dynamic

Patty and Andrew (from Chapter Ten) notice these two cycles in operation. In ordinary life it is Patty who tends to be the one who challenges and confronts. She is more likely to be operating in the growth cycle, whereas Andrew is more compliant, opting for more safety, avoiding issues that he doesn't know how to solve. Schnarch suggests that looking at their sexual relationship will show the patterns that operate in the wider relationship as well. When it comes to their sexual relationship is Andrew also tending to avoid confrontation, accepting what Patty wants? Or is he more willing to take some risks, telling Patty what it is that he likes?

The inner and outer cycles interact with each other – now pulling the relationship towards confrontation and growth – and the challenge of possible separation (or so it feels); and now pulling towards safety – and boredom and the status quo. It could be thought that the inner circle is the place of self-soothing, of safety. But real self-soothing is what takes place in the presence of confrontation. This is the 'holding on to oneself' that is necessary in the place of threat, and the call to growth.

Schnarch calls the sexual relationship and these processes the sexual crucible. A crucible is a vessel used as a melting pot, a place for fusing metal. Schnarch highlights the fact that our sexual relationship is a place of great challenge, and, as with the full relationship in which it is enfolded, really our only choice is to grow or stagnate. Either choice holds a risk of the relationship ending – growing and confronting may lead to termination by separating too much; choosing safety and therefore detachment leads to termination of the relationship by withdrawing into oneself too much. But the promise for those who persevere is of growth, maturity, becoming more of a whole person – in the context of a relationship which also grows as a result. Schnarch points out the need for holding on to myself, for self-soothing in order to stay committed to growth, in this most passionate of contexts: 'It's the crucible: Self-confrontation and self-soothing in the face of challenge; holding on to yourself. It's where your integrity is on the line.'[26]

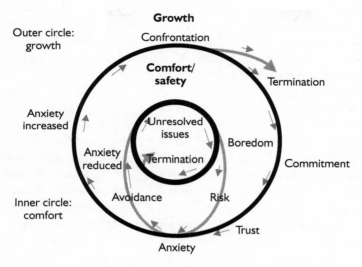

David Schnarch's Sexual Crucible

Schnarch's ideas are profound and deeply challenging. They are worthy of further exploration. His thesis is that relationships challenge us to become more individuated – more whole, more *myself* – by staying in connection with the other person. The connection itself will provoke me to know myself, to notice my differences, to become aware of my boundaries. Sexual relationships do this is in an intensified way because we are more sharply aware of our needs, our wants, our preferences. Our sexual encounters show us graphically whether we simply give in to the other, whether we state want we want, whether we are satisfied, whether we accept less than satisfaction, whether we will take risks. Sexual desire is so strong for most of us that it compels us to connect deeply with the other person – to say what we like and don't like, to ask for engagement, to overcome our differences and disagreements. In a short-term encounter we can avoid the honesty that is demanded in a long term relationship. A committed relationship creates the bridge which holds the risks and mistakes of sexual honesty – and therefore real individuation.

The sexual crucible demonstrates that relationships are always a paradox. On one side is the pull towards my defining of myself as an individual, confronting aspects of the relationship I am not happy with, the actions of the other person that concern me and, in contrast, my need for the safety of the relationship, the comfort it gives me, the refuge I find there. The danger of the latter is that I sacrifice my integrity, my sense of myself, in order to keep the peace and my sense of security. Most of us will tend to one or the other – more towards safety, or more towards confrontation – and the other person brings the balance. Either way the relationship is dynamic, alive, changing. The cost of safety is boredom, detachment, monotony. Our desire for real connection (whether sexual or otherwise) urges us to take risks – in the context of trust. Frequently women seek intimacy more than men do. This propels them back into relationship, to connecting, to sorting out differences. Men often want sex more regularly then their partners – this pushes them to engage with their partner, to reconnect when there has been a disagreement. Either way, the relationship dynamic pulls each person closer – and so can invite us to intimacy and integrity. This understanding of sex as a dynamic pull to honesty and real connection is key to committed sexual partnerships.

Try it

Focus on an intimate relationship – preferably a sexual one. Is your drive more towards confrontation, saying what you want; or more towards safety and keeping the peace? Can you voice what you want from the other person? Do you tend to compromise, in order to 'not upset' the status quo?

If the latter, can you articulate what you are afraid of? Is your relationship fun, life-giving, challenging? Are there ways you could inject life, with more honesty around what you want? Do you need to reassure the other person of your commitment so you can both take more risks? What action can you take? How can you share your understanding with your partner?

Eyes open

Schnarch is unusual as a sex therapist. Traditionally, sexual therapy has had a sensate focus – a focus on my physical experience, believing that this will help my body to arousal and responsiveness. In contrast, marriage counselling often emphasises improved communication – the interactions explored in Chapters Three and Four. While these are all part of the interface, Schnarch's focus is the dynamic of the intimate connection, the coming together of two individuating adults, the maturing that happens when two real people relate in honesty.

For many people, sex is about the physical experience; the ecstasy of orgasm, the warmth of being physically held. Most of us shut our eyes when we kiss, when we have intercourse – we focus in on the sensate pleasure. Or maybe we imagine being in another place or with another person. Our attention is on the physical feeling – and maybe on the giving of that physical pleasure to the other person. Either way it is sensate. And this indeed is the nature of sex. But it is also far more than this. For human beings sexual intimacy is about intimacy with *another person* – a sharing not only of my body but also of my soul. This may seem obvious but the reality is that most people experience sex – at least in the first years of relationship – as a physical ecstasy.

Old proverbs say that the eyes are the windows of the soul. When I look deeply into another person's eyes, I glimpse something of the real, inner person – and they see something of me. Schnarch's challenge is that we bring this into our sexual encounters, that we keep our eyes open during sex, that we experience orgasm not as an internal climax, but as an encounter with the other person – not someone I may be imagining in my own inner world, but the real person who is in relationship with me. This, he says, is the deepest challenge – to make each sexual encounter an opportunity for being seen for who I am without shame, seeing you for who you are with real appreciation.

Romance

Romantic love is one of the major compelling energies of the West. However irrelevant to the main plot, most movies will include a 'love interest'. A huge number of popular songs focus on romance, our longing for the other person, our need for a romantic partner. The thought of marrying someone for a reason other than romantic love is anathema to us. We find it hard to understand how arranged marriages could possibly have a higher success rate than love matches. And yet we also understand why someone may leave a long-term partner for someone new they have fallen in love with, as though the value of being in love is greater than anything else, including commitment, children, family. And the ecstasy of romantic love, especially coupled with sex, does feel, in the moment, as though anything else can be sacrificed in exchange.

Romantic love, like sex, heightens every aspect of the relationship – the attraction, the affirmation, the risks, the losses, the misunderstandings, the rejection. Our culture and socialization have so taught us that romantic love is the focal meaning, that any attraction is magnified, any rejection inflated, and the whole interaction fraught with potential danger – and excitement. We have inherited literature and romantic ideals from Shakespeare, Goethe and other writers from the Romantic era of the eighteenth and nineteenth centuries. The exalting of sentiment in these writings has left us with a residue of expectation that following whatever desires we have will lead to fulfilment.

Robert Johnson has explored this in his book *We: Understanding the Psychology of Romantic Love*. 'Romantic love is the single greatest energy system in the Western psyche. In our culture it has supplanted religion as the arena in which men and women seek meaning, transcendence, wholeness, and ecstasy.'[27] As a society, we have not yet learned to handle the tremendous power of romantic love. We turn it into tragedy and alienation as often as into enduring human relationships.

Romance and the Western psyche

To explore this transcendent desire of romantic love Robert
Johnson uses the myth of Tristan and Iseult: 'It is one of the most
moving, most beautiful and tragic of all the great epic tales. It was
the first story in Western literature that dealt with romantic love.
It is the source from which all our romantic literature has sprung,
from Romeo and Juliet down to the love story in the movie at the
local cinema... It shows a man torn among the conflicting forces
and loyalties that rage within the male psyche when he is consumed
by the joys, the passions, and the sufferings of romance.'[28]

The story of Tristan and Iseult dates from the time of the legends
of Arthur, the grail myths. King Marc of Cornwall needs a wife, and
Tristan, his nephew, seeks to bring him his bride. Through many
adventures Tristan eventually sails from Ireland back to Cornwall
with Iseult, the princess of this rival kingdom. On the way the ship
is becalmed, and while others go ashore Tristan and Iseult stay on
board in conversation. Getting thirsty, they look for a drink. They
find, unknowing, the love potion Iseult's mother has given to the
maid to be given to Marc and Iseult on their wedding night. They
drink, and fall in love – and cannot disentangle their souls for the
rest of their lives. The story becomes one of high romance, betrayal
and tragedy, Tristan and Iseult finally unite in death, having broken
their partners' hearts and shipwrecked their lives. And something
in our own hearts believes that it still was worth it, for the high
joy of romantic love.

The practices of other cultures suggest that, in contrast to our
present Western custom, marriages are often built on an initial
family agreement and the long slow love of commitment, sex,
friendship and family. Before the time of the Arthurian legends
– around 1200CE – marriages were more often of this kind, and
'romance' related to the stories of knights who went into battle for
a highborn lady, an inspiration to nobility and sacrifice, but not a
sexual partner. Over the centuries since, marriages were more and
more able to be based on mutual attraction, on romantic love, and
our songs and stories became woven through with this recurring
motif – the prince who woke Sleeping Beauty, Cinderella being

sought by the handsome prince, the Little Mermaid giving herself to pain so she could have legs and dance with her lover. These stories may sound like mere fairy stories – but the theme is repeated in our serious literature, our recurring myths of the hero who will give all for love, our loyalty and love of the 'People's Princess' whose wedding and funeral was followed by millions around the Western world.

Romance is deep in the heart of the Western psyche and we cannot easily escape it – nor do most of us want to. It seems to satisfy our core longings. The danger of course is that when it goes wrong we are devastated – it feels as though we have lost the meaning of life. The safeguards though are the same principles as we have already explored in previous chapters. Because of our idolizing of romantic love, it feels as though the principles of boundaries do not apply. There is a huge pull to merging our life with the other person. It seems as though 'becoming one' means that we lose our own personhood, rather than experiencing it as a call to more authentic selfhood and individuation.

In fact, the principles of boundaries and respect of the other person's boundaries need to be observed all the more. Romantic love can be a wonderful fairytale bridge to create connection, but needs the more mundane building blocks of self-awareness, owning our own feelings, 'I' statements, self disclosure, feedback, conflict resolution, apology and forgiveness to fashion a lasting bridge of enduring love.

One of the problems of romantic love is that it feels as though it should be exempt from the principles of 'ordinary' relationships. Our sense is that somehow it is in a different category. 'All's fair in love and war' expresses the idea that somehow the usual rules of relationship don't apply. 'Hell has no fury like a woman scorned', suggests that the betrayal of romantic love is worse than treason, murder maybe. The first successful legal plea of the 'grounds of insanity' for excusing of murder was an American member of Congress who shot his wife's lover in cold blood, (even though he had had many affairs himself).[29] The judge obviously accepted that the passion relating to a romantic relationship was in a special category.

Try it

What are your beliefs about romantic love?

How are your expectations of your romantic partner different from other relationships? Are you able to tell your romantic partner what your boundaries are, what your hopes are? Do you ever expect him/her to 'just know' what you want – or to remember what you have said without further reminder? Do you take offence more easily? Or blame more often?

What are the indicators that this person or relationship may have 'supplanted religion' – become an idol – a source of life-meaning?

Falling in love – the magic potion

The legend of Tristan and Iseult is an attempt of our culture to come to grips with the potency of sexual desire and romantic longing. When we struggle to understand we tend to make myths, stories which often contain magical elements to help us cope with the power and complexity of the ideas we are struggling with. In the story of Tristan and Iseult there are a number of magical events, the focal one being the drinking of the magic potion. We understand through the potion being magical, that Tristan and Iseult 'could not help' their being in love, even when Iseult was promised, then married, to someone else. We can excuse them because the potion was 'magic' and they were 'unable to resist it'.

Rosemary Sutcliff, the author of a number of books set in historic Britain, tells the story of Tristan and Iseult without the magic potion, because she challenges the idea that they were somehow different from us, that they could be excused for what they did. She makes the story more real to life – more like what we all might do. She explains:

> In all the versions that we know, Tristan and Iseult fall in love because they accidentally drink together a love potion which was meant for Iseult and her husband King Marc on

their wedding night. Now the story of Tristan and Iseult
is basically the same as two other great Celtic love stories,
Diarmid and Grania, and Deirdre and the sons of Usna, and
in neither of them is there any suggestion of a love potion.
I am sure in my own mind that the medieval storytellers
added it to make an excuse for Tristan and Iseult for
being in love with each other when Iseult was married
to somebody else. And for me, this turns something that
was real and living and part of themselves into something
artificial, the result of drinking a sort of magic drug. So I
have left out the love potion.[30]

Rosemary Sutcliff is helping us face the reality of human
sexuality – that our passion, our being in love, and sexual contact
is such a strong compulsion that it is difficult to resist, – but it is
not magic, it is very human. So when Sutcliff tells of Tristan and
Iseult falling in love she uses the catalyst of touch, and romantic
imagery and helps us identify with the sexual-romantic longing
which has become part of our culture.

Now this was the first time that ever they had touched
each other, save for the times when the Princess had tended
Tristan's wounds, and that was a different kind of touching;
and as he set her down, their hands came together as
though they did not want it to be so quickly over. And
standing hand in hand, they looked at each other, and
for the first time Tristan saw that the Princess's eyes were
deeply blue, the colour of wild wood-columbines; and she
saw that his were as grey as the restless water out beyond
the headland. And they were so close that each saw their
own reflection standing in the other one's eyes; and in that
moment it was as though something of Iseult entered into
Tristan and something of Tristan into Iseult, that could
never be called back again for as long as they lived.[31]

Sutcliff uses romantic language – and finishes the telling of the encounter with a powerful image – something of each person entered the other and could not be called back. Such is the profound bonding of romantic and sexual love in a culture which has made romance a peak experience of ecstasy. And the implication is that 'we can't help it', we can't stop ourselves falling in love – it just happens to us, like the unknowing drinking of a magic potion. (We will explore this further in the next chapter.)

One of the problems with the West's embracing of romance as a substitute for religion is simply that it usually doesn't work. And we become disappointed and disillusioned if we are unable to make the shift to the reality of our partner being as human as we are. Freud, who made sex so central to study of the psyche, in his own life was disappointed in his expectations. 'The spiritual disillusionment and bodily deprivation to which most marriages are thus doomed puts both partners back in the state they were in before their marriage, except for being the poorer by the loss of an illusion.'[32] Freud's statement shows his own disillusionment around sex – but does not point to another more satisfying focus. Carl Jung, on the other hand, an earlier follower of Freud, who then developed his understanding of humanness along other lines, saw spirituality as the more appropriate focus for maturity.

It feels to us as though sex and romance should have different rules. All I am really saying in this chapter is that 'the same rules apply.' It just doesn't feel like it. But in the end all relationships work by the same principles – and this whole book is about sexual and romantic relationships in that sense.

13

Spirituality, Shadow, Dreams and Self

Me and not me in complex places

One of the complexities of being in relationship is working out what is me and what is not me – what belongs to me and what belongs to the relationship. My emotional reactions are my own, but how I react to my partner's emotional reactions and their pain or excitement or desire are also part of the relationship. In this chapter I want to explore spirituality, shadow and dreams – all of which are largely 'mine' but which also impact on my relationships. My spirituality is my belief system or my relationship with the Divine – clearly within my boundaries – but it impacts on how I relate to others. My shadow, the part of myself I do not acknowledge, is also within my boundaries (though in my blind-spots); but again will impact on my relationships, maybe puzzling other people by its seeming inconsistency. My dreams and my sense of self are my own – but affect, and are affected by, my relationships with those around me.

Joanne and Tim have been together for some years. They have both been working but have now decided to have a family and share the parenting. They are wondering how this life transition will affect their relationship. Joanne was brought up in a Catholic family but stopped going to church when she left home and went to university. 'It really didn't have any meaning for me', she said. 'And I don't want my children to be scared by stories of sin and hell.' Tim had no childhood religion, but is attracted to some of the ideas of Buddhist spirituality. The challenge of this life transition is making them wonder how spirituality may be part of their relationship or the lives of their children.

Spirituality is the awareness that there is something more than the material world. Each culture develops a spirituality – myths, gods or God, a morality grounded in something beyond the physical world. The postmodernism of the West is questioning the traditional Judeo-Christian worldview, rejecting legalism and fundamentalism, opting for a more open, individual exploration of the meaning of life, the transcendent, spiritual practices.

Joanne and Tim are typical of young adults of the twenty-first century – questioning the 'religion' – or lack of it – that was part of their childhood, they are wondering what their own spirituality might be. Tim is an art teacher and has always felt the pull to spirituality through his appreciation of beauty in visual art, and through music. He likes the idea of spirituality that is linked to the beauty of the earth. Joanne is realizing that her relationship with Tim gave meaning to her life after she left home. Rejecting the religion of her childhood, she found significance and purpose in her romance. 'At first, starting a new life with Tim meant everything to me', she admits. 'You could say he was my Romeo. My mother had wanted me to find a Catholic boy, but she understood me being in love with Tim. She really likes him – fortunately! – but I know she still hopes we'll bring our children up in the church. That's not for me though. But I have to admit that now we're settling down and having a family, well, I wonder if there isn't something more.'

Joanne and Tim are making the transition from finding the meaning of life in each other. While romance may have felt like the be all and end all, they are now more accepting of each other's humanity. They want to give their children some kind of spiritual meaning but don't want to be tied down to dogma and doctrine.

While spirituality can be intensely personal, it also impacts on relationships, especially romantic relationships, in our culture. Joanne is recognizing that Tim 'meant everything' to her. It may be that Tim also found meaning through her. Like Tristan in the myth, he may have unconsciously taken his love for her as his guiding light, his reason for killing dragons. Now they are both at a point in their lives where the love potion has worn off. They still love each other and are deeply committed to that love, to a future together with children and a family life. Their love has changed – it has become the more solid stuff of everyday interaction. The expectation of continuous fireworks and happily-ever-after has changed to the give and take of realistic expectations and acceptance of each other's humanness. What happens now, to the longing for something bigger, the haunting love-sickness that entice humans to be always looking for something greater? Rilke, the German poet, wrote of the great homesickness we could never shake off.[33] The challenge for Tim and Joanne is to find a spirituality, rather than insisting that their partner fulfils that place in their lives – or, more dangerously, that another romantic partner should do so.

Masculine, feminine – and how not to fall in love

If Tim, for example, does not make the shift from expecting romance and sex to satisfy his deeper longings, then the following scenario may well play out. Joanne is pregnant – very happily so – but with the usual ups and downs of emotions and physical changes. For a time she is not interested in sex. Meanwhile a new teacher starts at Tim's school. Megan is teaching art and drama, she's young and attractive, intelligent and vivacious. She has a dramatic and emotional breakup with her boyfriend and one afternoon turns to Tim for understanding.

If Tim is still drawn by the myth of being a knight in shining armour – one who kills dragons and rescues maidens – he's on dangerous territory. If he is disappointed in Joanne no longer looking at him as adoringly as she used to, and he has not learned how to find his significance in something bigger than he is, in a spirituality, then he is vulnerable to an affair. And if he believes that drinking the magic potion is something that 'just happens', then indeed it might 'just happen'.

However, it is possible to prevent ourselves falling in love. It just has to be done before we jump on the toboggan – the runaway vehicle that is already moving. If Tim finds Megan attractive – and it's unlikely he wouldn't – then he needs to put some safeguards in place.

One safeguard is to agree – early in the relationship if possible – to tell your partner about who you are attracted to. Even in the early days of their romance, when he and Joanne were madly in love, it is likely he was attracted to other women. Telling Joanne is a powerful way to defuse the magnetism to others. For a woman the attractions may be different. I found I was likely to be drawn to men who had some kind of authority or power – especially if they seemed to notice me as a woman. I made a practice of telling my husband of my attraction. His usual response was, 'Well that's natural.' It neutralized the potency of the temptation – allowing me to be open and honest. Secrecy has its own special power.

Another safeguard is to form a relationship with the partner of someone I am attracted to. I am much less likely to cheat on a friend. To see a person I am attracted to as one of a couple helps reinforce that they are not available, and respecting their partner helps me respect their relationship. Work relationships are particularly vulnerable because we work together with someone, finding common ground with them – and seldom relate to their partner. Professional roles and principles can help keep the distance also. It may be that Tim could use this approach, 'Megan I'm a teaching colleague, we need to keep the relationship on that level. I know the school counsellor will know someone you can see.' It sounds terribly ungallant, but right now Tim's first responsibility is his wife. And having an affair with Megan is certainly not going to rescue her effectively.

As Rosemary Sutcliff's telling of the Tristan and Iseult myth made plain, touch – and a belief in romantic love as a peak experience – leaves us wide open to enchantment and tragedy. If Tim and Joanne can continue to be honest with each other about their longings, their attractions, their sexual desires, their love for each other, their relationship is more likely to survive the storms of life. If Tim discovers, as Schnarch has elaborated, that a sexual relationship with a long term partner can be far more satisfying than a short term excitement, then his relationship with Joanne is on steady ground.

Frequently, the people we are attracted to romantically and sexually are those who somehow represent something we are not acknowledging in ourselves. It is usual, in young love at least, to be attracted most to a person who somehow embodies something lacking in ourselves. This is projection, the process whereby we 'project' our own intention, fear, desire on to someone else (as discussed in Chapter Eleven).

Masculine and feminine attracted to each other

If Tim falls in love with Megan he is likely seeing in her her femininity, idealism, sensitivity, vulnerability, creativity – all qualities which he himself possesses but maybe cannot acknowledge in himself. Part of growing up is the invitation to develop the qualities we have called feminine, within the masculine; to develop the qualities we call the masculine, within the feminine. In the first half of life at least, we usually see the other gender qualities in the other person – rather than in ourselves – and so fall in love with them, wanting the other person to complete us. In other words, it is easy for a male to see a woman as soft, kind, responsive, other-centred and tender and to be attracted to that, unconsciously bringing the 'feminine' into himself by joining himself to her. And it is easy for a woman to be attracted to the 'masculine' – strength, initiative, protectiveness, rationality – and find it by joining herself to a man. Of course, this is oversimplifying the dynamic, but it is a common place to start. These are stereotypes. None of us are all-masculine, or all-feminine. We all have a unique mix. But in adolescence it can feel as though we are expected to be a particular 'correct' mix – or to be only one gender. The call to maturity is a call to developing the masculine in the feminine, the feminine in the masculine, not being afraid to develop all the qualities which make up the unique person I am to be 'fully alive'.

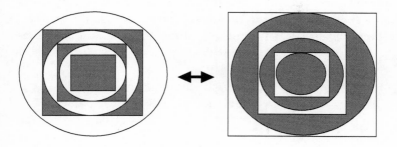

Developing the feminine in the masculine, the masculine in the feminine

As we get older and more aware of this dynamic, a romantic attraction should alert us to the fact that we are projecting – and therefore what we need to be looking for in ourselves. Rather than simply 'male attracts female', there is a complicated mix which attracts the other person. Numbers of theorists and therapists, including Harville Hendrix in *Getting the Love you Want*,[34] suggest that there is chemistry between a couple when the other person unconsciously reminds us of something unresolved from our childhood. We will continually be attracted to the same kind of person until we do the emotional work we need to do to resolve it within ourselves. Frequently, the person we are attracted to reminds us in some (often hidden) way of our opposite sex parent. The work we need to do is to develop the hidden qualities within ourselves. This is sometimes called 'shadow' work.

Shadow

In the same way that all of us have a physical shadow, we all have a psychological shadow, parts of us that we may not be aware of. The shadow is not the 'bad' parts of us. Rather, it is the hidden, unacknowledged part. Often it is made up of parts that were not acceptable to our parents, or to society in general. It could be gentleness in a boy, independence in a girl, outspokenness in a compliant family, intuitiveness in a practical family, spirituality in a non-religious family. Any quality at all can become shadow – and is frequently a part of our giftedness. There is 'gold in the shadow', as Jung explained it. Therapist and author Robert Johnson explains the development of the shadow like this:

> somewhere early on our way... things separate into good and evil, and we begin the shadow-making process; we divide our lives... we sort out our God-given characteristics into those that are acceptable to our society and those that have to be put away... But the refused and unacceptable characteristics do not go away; they only collect in the dark corners of our personality. When they have been hidden long enough they take on a life of their own – the shadow life.[35]

Shadow awareness is important for our relationships because it helps us become conscious of a part of ourselves which will otherwise seem intrusive, capricious, 'out of character.' If we only see each other as the face that is shown to the outside world, we will miss the deeper, more hidden, but just-as-real parts of each other.

One of the ways we can become aware of shadow is to recognize these 'out of character' reactions. They will appear particularly when we are under stress, and they are most likely to be seen by the people we love and trust. The kind of event that makes us say, 'I don't know what came over me! I was beside myself!' The mild-mannered tortoise of Chapter Ten suddenly turns into a shark when her children are threatened. These 'out of character' reactions are in fact part of our character, and will have a consistency about them, in the same way that our personality does. The concept of shadow, in fact, suggests that these out of character parts of us will be the 'underside' of our everyday personality. Naomi Quenk, in *Beside Ourselves*,[36] explores the idea that the opposite, or inferior side of our personality, can burst out unexpectedly. Rather than seeing it as some weird aberration, helping each other accept this side of us, can allow us to become more balanced and whole.

Another pointer to shadow is forgetting. Of course all of us forget – forget to do something, forget we had promised something, forget what we were going to buy or what we were going to say. It is worth noticing what we forget – especially if it is repeated. We often forget something we don't really want to do, or something that threatens us in some way. Another version of this is to notice the things we don't have time to do. We might not actually have forgotten – we just ran out of time. It was never priority. It is another clue to what is hidden in the shadow, what we are resisting at an unconscious level.

Another very creative way to discovering shadow is to notice our dreams.

Dreams

Freud called dreams the 'royal road to the unconscious'. His work and that of Carl Jung have enabled us to make sense of dreams which otherwise may appear bizarre, irrelevant, laughable. It seems that our brain is busy during sleep carrying out integrative work. This can be likened to the 'defrag' process of computers – bringing sense and meaning from the fragments of our everyday life. What may at first appear as bizarre and weird can be incredibly creative representations of parts of ourselves which are otherwise hidden.

I remember hearing a missionary lady telling of a dream she had had while overseas with her cross-cultural mission organization. In the dream she was walking along the road with a fellow worker when she suddenly started bashing him over the head and saying, 'I hate you, I hate you.' On waking, this kind and mild-mannered woman was finally able to admit her 'un-Christian' frustration with the man she worked with. Her husband, waking beside her, asked what was the matter. She began to tell him and the realization hit her, 'And I hate you too!'.

Our dreams can allow us to see the shadow parts of ourselves because they expose our feelings, sometimes in nightmare colour, and make us face the reality of what is going on under the surface of our lives. The pictures of our dreams are often symbols, like cryptic crossword clues, using metaphors and even puns to make us tease out the meaning underneath.

Making sense of dreams

One of the basic principles of dreams is that every person in the dream is myself. While dreams can tell me about my side of a relationship, and how I am feeling, they are not about the other person – they are about me. If the missionary woman was to go to the fellow worker and say to him, 'In my dream you were arguing with me, I want you to tell me what you disagree with me about', she would be missing the point and misinterpreting the dream.

The way to interpret other people in my dream is to ask myself what qualities that person has. I once dreamed I had locked my administration officer, a woman, into a suitcase. Why that particular woman? What qualities did I notice most in her? Her orderliness, her attention to detail, her ability to get on with her work in an objective way. The relevant question for me was how had I locked up these qualities in myself. I also have the ability to be detailed, ordered, objective – but that is not my dominant work mode. How was I locking up these qualities? In the dream I was afraid that I had starved this woman in the suitcase. How was I starving myself? How was I refusing to nurture the more ordered side of myself? The dream was not about my administration officer – it was about me, the 'administration-officer' side of myself.

A person of the same gender in a dream is frequently a shadow quality of myself, a part of myself I am not acknowledging or valuing. How was I locking up this part of myself? How was I not even acknowledging it? What would it be like to acknowledge this part of myself? What might I be afraid would happen if I unlocked it?

For women, then, another woman in a dream often represents a shadow part of myself – whatever quality that particular person represents to me. And for a man, another man in his dream, represents a shadow part, an unacknowledged part of himself. Dreaming of his son may be an invitation to look at the younger, more playful or more immature part of himself. Dreaming of a murderer would be invitation to acknowledge his own anger or repressed tendency to violence.

For women, a man in a dream can represent the masculine in herself. The missionary woman's dream-self telling her co-worker she hates him may well be an indication that she hates the masculine part of herself. A good Christian missionary woman may well have had reason to hide and denigrate the masculine part of herself. It may well have been difficult for her in that context to be a woman who could happily take the initiative, to be decisive and directive.

For a man, a woman in his dream can represent his own feminine side. A romantic conversation with a beautiful woman in a dream may at first simply be seen as showing his sexual desire. But at a deeper level it is an invitation for a man to be more in touch with his own feminine element, the beauty within himself.

Another important principle in understanding dreams is that there is no morality. That is, what I do in a dream is not 'wrong' – it is a story, a picture – a way of telling me more about myself. The missionary woman did not have to make amends for her violence in the dream – the violence was simply revealing her inner feelings to her. She did not actually 'do' anything wrong. Violence in a dream is not 'wrong' – it is simply exposing to us our strong reactions. Extra-marital sex is not 'wrong' in dreams – it is just revealing to us our fears and our desires – our need for integration. Murder is not 'wrong' – but it is a strong indicator I need to do something about some strong feelings! – some shadow work. And if we don't listen to our dreams, they repeat, or become nightmares, to catch our attention. Nightmares are, as a colleague of mine says, 'dreams with the volume turned up.'

Self

The topics explored in this chapter are parts of our selves and therefore parts of our relationships, but primarily within my own boundaries. My self and my sense of my self impact my relationships – but they are my responsibility, not the responsibility of the people I am in relationships with.

My sense of self will be largely determined by my childhood experiences – and then altered somewhat by life's experiences and relationships. Audrey, in Chapter One, was sexually abused as a child. It is very likely that her sense of self will be deeply affected, and will need concerted emotional work on her part to change. She may well have a sense of herself as a victim, someone who cannot choose what she wants, and who must comply with other people's demands of her. Even though someone may fall in love with her and tell her she is wonderful, she will find it hard to believe, may even reject their love, be suspicious of their motives, or, in over-reaction, give herself without reserve – and without boundaries. Becoming a 'self' for Audrey – and all of us – involves getting to know what we like and what we don't like, what we want and what we don't want, what gives us pleasure, what we are afraid of, what we aspire to. Frequently this coming to know ourselves happens in the context of relationships. It is often in having people cross our boundaries that we realise a boundary is there. It is in someone else choosing what we don't want that we are stimulated to name what we do want.

While some people have an undeveloped sense of self, others have an inflated sense of self. According to a biography of Mao Tse Tung, Mao was indulged by his mother and other female relatives in whose extended family he lived until he was eight. Mao seems to have grown up with a sense of self that put him outside the usual human moral constraints, letting him do what he liked whatever effect it had on other people. In his twenties he wrote notes about morality which seem to have guided him for the rest of his life: 'I do not agree with the view that to be moral, the motives of one's action has to be benefiting others... Of course there are people and objects in the world, but they are all there only for me.'[37] In all, seventy million people died during Mao's rulership – in peacetime.

Having a realistic sense of self is the result of being open to feedback, not so that others will dictate to me what I should be, but so that I gain an understanding of how my behaviour affects other people. I remember as a teenager puzzling over whether I was who I saw myself to be, or who other people perceived me to be. In fact I am both – and neither. My blind spots, and other people's subjective perceptions, mean that we each see through a distorted glass. In the final analysis I am the one responsible for who I am – but I can do with all the help I can get from trustworthy friends along the way.

One of the important ways to develop my sense of self is to be able to identify my needs. An important way to keep a relationship 'sustainable' is to be able to voice the realities of who I am and what my needs are. This is the subject of the final chapter.

14

Sustainable Relationships

Building relationships to last

Andrew and Patty in Chapter Ten were discovering their conflict styles – and at the same time learning to be more honest about their own needs and wants. As Patty learned to say that she needed Andrew to respond to her preferences – rather than those of her parents – she was able to articulate what she wanted more honestly.

There is a difference between needs, wants and preferences. There are few things that we absolutely need for survival. But for the survival of a relationship it is useful to be able to tell our friend, colleague or partner what our preferences are, as well as to be able to identify what is such a strong preference that it is a need. It may be helpful on some occasions to be able to say, 'My preference is that we get the task finished by this weekend, but I need it for sure to be finished by the middle of next week.' 'My preference is that your mother stays in a motel rather than in our apartment, but if you really want her to come, then my need would be that she only stays with us for three days maximum. Or alternatively I could go away for a few days and let you and her have some time together.' Being able to differentiate preferences at one end of the continuum, and needs at the other, gives our partner useful information. For the rest of this chapter, however, I will use the term needs so the focus can be about communication and boundaries, rather than the strength of the preference.

Many of us have thought, like Andrew, that a good relationship is about giving in to the needs of a partner, unless we feel very strongly and so claim what we want. Relationships work more effectively, however, when both partners feel free to express their needs and negotiate what is important for them. When this is a mutual process the relationship can develop in a healthy way. It is when the relationship is lopsided that difficulties arise. Often, during the 'honeymoon' initial phase of a relationship, two people are willing to go along with the other person's needs without demur. After this phase though, more negotiation will have to take place, and if one person is afraid, or socialized in such a way that they think they should not express needs, then the relationship becomes vulnerable to sabotage.

Joanne and Tim, in Chapter Thirteen, are in a vulnerable place right now. It is important that Tim is able to express his needs to Joanne – even though he may dismiss this thinking, believing that she needs to be protected or sheltered at present. If he does not express his needs, though, he is vulnerable to falling in to another relationship.

Expressing my needs

Expressing my needs openly is a way to protect the relationship – to keep within the relationship what should be within its boundaries. If we do not acknowledge our needs we are almost certain to seek their fulfilment, either consciously or unconsciously, somewhere else. Expressing our needs in the context of the relationship is an important way of being vulnerable, of building trust and of inviting the support of the other person.

Another important outcome of learning to express our needs is that it clarifies whose needs are whose. We frequently fool ourselves about whose needs we are meeting. When I ask myself 'Whose needs?' I clarify the boundaries. I want my daughter to learn the violin, even though she is not very interested right now. Is this for her sake so she will gain a musical appreciation – or is it mine, because I want to impress my mother that I am educating my daughter in a way my mother would want? Persuading my elderly mother to buy a new oven when she is content with her old one begs the question, 'Whose needs?' Is it for my mother's safety – or for my need, so I don't worry about her? If I tell my son not to try a certain trick on his skateboard – 'Whose needs?' His – to be safe; or mine – not to feel anxious. So what if he breaks his arm? Where are the boundaries of safety for him, for me?

My partner's mother wants to come and stay. Whose needs? Hers? My partner's? It is not that there are right and wrong answers – rather it is about clarifying the boundaries so that decisions can be made in openness.

Try it

Choose one of your most important relationships. Name your most important needs within that relationship. Right now – what is it that you most want/need from the other person? Do you have any hesitations about talking about these needs? Has the other person given you reason to believe you cannot name these needs? Can you identify what their needs would be if they were to name them?

Think of a way to talk with this person about your needs – and their needs.

Voice

We have probably all endured the rather disconcerting experience of losing our voice – a cold or other virus takes away our ability to speak for a day or two, and we are left floundering and feeling powerless. Even more disconcerting is 'losing our voice' in a psychological way. This might be in a meeting where everyone is agreeing and we disagree but are caught by surprise and don't know what to say. Or in a relationship where the other person is insisting on their perspective and we feel powerless to express a different viewpoint. Afterwards we may well think of many clever or reasonable arguments, but for the moment we were stuck, and voiceless.

In the 1980s a rather interesting study was done about how people knew what was true – how they came to know what they did. From the study, a small group of participants were identified and given the designation 'silent', because they couldn't identify what was true, did not know how to express ideas or who to believe. They were women who had been abused and consequently felt of no worth – they did not even feel that they could identify what they knew.

The results of the study were published in *Women's Ways of Knowing*,[38] which described various other groups and ways of knowing also. The response to the book surprised the authors by the very high level of interest. One particular point especially surprised them. It was the number of people who identified with the silent group, the women with no voice. Even well-educated people, including those in positions of authority, contacted the authors and told them how they also knew what it was like to be without a voice, to have their power taken away – the simple power of being able to give voice to what they wanted to say.

Voice is the freedom to say what you want to say without fear of reprisal. It is about the quality of the relationship – the agreement between two or more people, that each can express what they want, and they will be listened to. If my partner will laugh at me if I say what I need, my voice is taken away. If I fear my boss will be against me if I venture criticism, my voice is taken away. If my ideas, thoughts, preferences are disregarded over and over, eventually my ability to speak withers up.

Most of us experience at least one relationship where we feel we 'cannot say anything.' My parents, my boss, my partner. The no-go areas. 'Oh I couldn't tell him that. He just won't listen.' 'I've tried and tried to talk to her about it. I just don't say anything now.' 'He just refuses to talk about it.' In most cases it is not that the person *actually* cannot speak about it, it is rather a tacit agreement not to; a psychological buffer, defences forming a barrier, emotional gridlock.

The agreement between two people that openness is a joint value has to be very strong. Perhaps an agreement between two partners to talk once a week about their needs. Perhaps a meeting with the boss, and a third party if need be, to voice ideas and possibilities. Maybe a gathering of several people with the stated valuing of and commitment to hearing each other. The reiteration of the value is needed because our defences will otherwise silence the other person.

Try it

Think of an example where you wanted to say something but 'lost your voice.' What factors caused the silencing? With hindsight, would you be able to act differently if you could relive this incident?
Identify the relationships that are most important to you. What issues or topics do you find it difficult to talk about? What would it be like to be able to talk honestly?
How could you take one step towards 'finding voice' in this relationship?

If the relationship is between people where one has more power, that person in particular has to reinforce their commitment to listening, to valuing the voice of the other. Frequently the person with more power is unaware of the way they deny the voice of the other/s. It is part of their blind spot, part of the shadow that all of us live with. Many husbands are unaware that their wives are unhappy – until the wife leaves. She thinks she told him – but he wouldn't listen. Her experience was that her voice had been taken away. Similarly, in organizations, people finally end up giving notice – and the boss has little idea of what he could have done differently.

If a person experiences the other as having more power, or as 'closing them down', they feel silenced, voiceless. Giving the other person voice involves an explicit invitation to speak, and then listening – and saying what has been heard to check if it is heard correctly and fully.

His needs, her needs

In his book *His Needs, Her Needs*,[39] psychologist and marriage counsellor Willard Harley explains how he started asking couples what they needed from their partner to make them happy. He found that in general the top needs of husbands and wives are different. Men value a sexual relationship, recreational companionship and admiration. Women need affection, openness and honesty, conversation, a good father to their children. Your needs may be different from those Harley lists, but the point is that we tend to assume that our partner has the same values and wants that we do. Long-term relationships need a place to voice needs and preferences – and a responsive partner. A real partnership is not about one person sacrificing themselves for the others' needs, but is about each person knowing the safety of a commitment from the other person to hear and allow them voice.

When Patty asks Andrew what it is he wants, she doesn't want him to just go along with her. The difficulty is, of course, that she may not want to hear what he wants either, if it means compromising! And because she is more articulate – as many women are when it comes to emotional and relational matters – she may be able to make Andrew feel silly – in fact, to silence him, without realizing she is doing it. The bridge of their love and commitment to each other is necessary to enable them both to continue to voice their needs.

Voice and equality – another model for organizations

This commitment to valuing honesty is more difficult in organizations, because there is not a sustained bridge of honesty and love to hold the relationship. Nevertheless the principle still holds – that being *for* each other, being committed to hearing each other, will bring about the most effective and lasting relationships. The principle of a side by side relating explored in Chapter Seven, as opposed to a top-down, over-against relationship has implications for organizations and group relationships also.

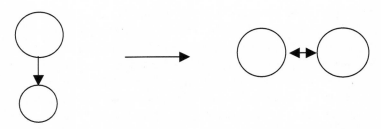

Over-against, top down   Side by side, equal

If people in an organization or group are committed to valuing effective relationships, they will need to investigate what it means to develop these kinds of relationships in spite of organizational structure and role requirements. Living in an over–against or top-down relationship leads to a hierarchical understanding of relationship, because comparison and therefore ranking are implicit in the evaluation paradigm of Chapter Seven.

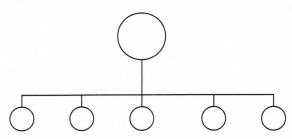

The top-down, organizational chart authority line concepts fit hand in glove with the evaluation paradigm. They may help with organizational effectiveness but they work against relationship effectiveness unless there is explicit commitment to voice, honesty and equality. We need to explore alternatives to value each person's gifts and most effective contribution.

One example of a different way of thinking about organizational relationships is the more organic picture of a body – made up of different, but equally important parts. The body functions together, valuing all its parts for the good of all. The role of the manager, in this model, is seen as a functional one – not a hierarchical one. As a manager my gift is to look at the whole picture and to see how the parts will fit together most effectively. As I meet with my team, it is so I can contribute my understanding to the whole picture, and so the others can share their perspectives with me. This is admittedly a much more challenging way of relating than in hierarchy – which is why we so often revert to hierarchical relationships. Relating together as equals requires more commitment to honesty, openness and vulnerability.

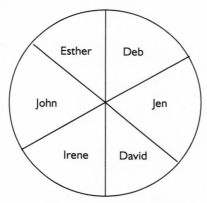

A more equal model for organizational relationships

Ideals and reality

I tend to be an idealistic person. If I can imagine it, I want to make it happen. I can remember when I was about nineteen discussing with a friend our belief that we could be perfect. I expected that in a few years I would be perfect and I would get on with fixing the world. Not many people are as idealistic as I was.

Now in my fifties, I am more realistic – and more gentle with myself too. Many of the ideas I have explored in the preceding chapters are about ideals – the best possibilities. I now understand that the best I'm going to get is an imperfect relationship between imperfect people – and that's the way the world is. But it leaves a lot more room for forgiveness and space to try again, to learn slowly and to be kind to each other on the way – and to have a few deep friendships.

References

1 John Powell, *Why Am I Afraid to Tell You Who I Am?*, Notre Dame, IN: Thomas More (1969).

2 Augusten Burroughs, *Running With Scissors: A Memoir*, New York: St Martin's Press (2002).

3 Henry Cloud and John Townsend, *Boundaries: When to Say Yes, How to Say No, to Take Control of Your Life*, Grand Rapids, MI: Zondervan (1995).

4 Nelson Mandela, *A Long Walk to Freedom: The Autobiography of Nelson Mandela*, London: Abacus (1994), p. 444.

5 Albert Gelpi, *Living in Time: The Poetry of C. Day Lewis*, Oxford: Oxford University Press (1998), p. 215.

6 J. Luft and H. Ingham, 'The Johari Window, a Graphic Model of Interpersonal Awareness', in *Proceedings of the Western Training Laboratory in Group Development*, Los Angeles: UCLA (1955).

7 Mark Haddon, *The Curious Incident of the Dog in the Night-time*, New York: Doubleday (2003), p. 3.

8 D. Siegel, 'Evolution of Psychotherapy' conference, Los Angeles, December 2005.

9 Eric Berne, *The Games People Play: The Psychology of Human*

Relationships, New York: Ballantine (1973).

10 For example see Richard Rohr, *Adam's Return: The Five Promises of Male Initiation*, New York: Crossroad (2004).

11 M. Scott Peck, *The Road Less Travelled*, London: Arrow (1983).

12 M. Scott Peck, *A World Waiting to be Born: Civility Rediscovered*, New York: Bantam (1993).

13 Harriet Lerner, *The Dance of Connection: How to Talk to Someone When You Are Mad, Hurt, Scared, Frustrated, Insulted, Betrayed or Desperate*, New York: HarperCollins (2001).

14 John M. Gottman and Nan Silver, *The Seven Principles for Making Marriage Work: A Practical Guide from the Country's Foremost Marriage Expert*, New York: Three Rivers (1999), p. 80.

15 'Municipalité Hérouxville', from http://municipalite. herouxville.qc.ca/Standards.pdf

16 Gary Chapman, *The Five Love Languages*, Chicago: Northfield (1995).

17 Stephen Mitchell, *Tao Te Ching: A New English Version*, New York: Harper Perennial (2000), p. 7.

18 Harriet Lerner, *The Dance of Anger: A Woman's Guide to Changing the Patterns of Intimate Relationships,* New York: HarperCollins (1997).

19 David Schnarch, *Passionate Marriage: Love, Sex and Intimacy in Emotionally Committed Relationships*, New York: Norton (1997).

20 Stephen R. Covey, *The Seven Habits of Highly Effective People*, New York: Simon and Schuster (1989).

21 Eric Segal, *Love Story*, New York: Harper and Row (1970).

22 Robert J. Sternberg, *The Triangle of Love: Intimacy, Passion, Commitment*, New York: Basic Books (1988).

23 Robert J. Sternberg and Michael J. Barnes, eds, *The Psychology of Love*, New Haven, CT: Yale University Press (1988), p. 121.

24 Robert J. Sternberg, *Love is a Story: A New Theory of Relationships*, Oxford: Oxford University Press (1998).

25 David Schnarch, *Passionate Marriage,* p. 355.

26 David Schnarch, *Passionate Marriage,* p. 356.

27 Robert A. Johnson, *We: Understanding the Psychology of Romantic Love*, San Francisco: Harper (1985), p. xi.

28 Robert A. Johnson, *We*, p. xiv.

29 Thomas Keneally, *American Scoundrel: The Life of the Notorious Civil War General Dan Sickles*, London: Serpentine (2002).

30 Rosemary Sutcliff, *Tristan and Iseult*, London: The Bodley Head (1971), pp. 7–8.

31 Rosemary Sutcliff, *Tristan and Iseult*, pp. 60–61.

32 Sigmund Freud, "'Civilised' sexual morality and modern nervous illness'", cited in Louis Hudson and Bernadine Jacot, *The Way Men Think: Intellect, Intimacy and the Erotic Imagination*, New Haven, CT: Yale University (1991), p. 4.

33 Rainer Maria Rilke, *Rilke's Book of Hours: Love Poems to God*, ed. and trans. Anita Barrows and Joanna Marie Macy, New York: Riverhead (1996), p. 70.

34 Harville Hendrix, *Getting the Love You Want: A Guide for Couples*, New York: Henry Holt (2001).

35 Robert A. Johnson, *Owning Your Own Shadow.* San Francisco: Harper (1993), p. 14.

36 Naomi L. Quenk, *Beside Ourselves: Our Hidden Personality in Everyday Life*, Mountain View, CA: Consulting Psychologists Press (1993).

37 Jon Halliday and Jung Chang, *Mao: The Unknown Story*, New York: Knopf (2005). p. 13.

38 Mary Belenky, Blythe Clinchy, Nancy Goldberger and Jill Tarule, *Women's Ways of Knowing: The Development of Self, Voice, and Mind*, New York: Basic Books (1986).

39 Willard Harley, *His Needs, Her Needs: Building an Affair-proof Marriage,* Grand Rapids, MI: Revell (1986).

More titles from Lion:

THE ENNEAGRAM: A PRIVATE SESSION WITH
THE WORLD'S GREATEST PSYCHOLOGIST
Simon Parke

The Enneagram is a time-honoured way of understanding
personality types and human behaviour. It is both ancient
and modern. Developed over 1500 years by both Sufi
and Christian mystics, it was overhauled in the twentieth
century by the disciplines and insights of Western
psychology. It identifies nine types of personality, describes
the ways they interrelate, and is widely used today as a
perceptive guide to self-understanding.

In this original and enticing book, 'Enneagram' unveils his
insights in the form of letters to and from enquirers. These
finely-drawn portraits of the nine faces of humanity will
not only give you a deeper understanding of who you are,
but will also guide you through the complex inner world
of others.

**'There is no better guide to this fascinating subject
than Simon Parke. You'd be stupid to miss it.'**
Simon Mayo

ISBN: 978-0-7459-5314-4

EMOTIONAL PROCESSING:
HEALING THROUGH FEELING
Dr Roger Baker

Is there a way of harnessing our emotions, of living in harmony with them and finding meaning and fulfilment through them?

In *Emotional Processing*, Dr Roger Baker offers a new psychological approach. Basing his writing on twenty years of experience in therapy and the groundbreaking research he has undertaken with his research team, he explains how emotional processing works.

He begins by examining the meaning and purpose of emotions, affirming the crucially important role they play in a full and healthy life. They are, he says, an advanced information system, not an opponent of rational thought. He then goes on to show how we have a sort of second immune system, able to absorb and break down emotional hurts and stress just as our first immune system deals with viruses and bacteria. When we move with this system of emotional processing, instead of blocking or hindering it, life's troubles and traumas can be so much more easily absorbed.

Illustrated throughout with examples from patients in psychological therapy and from everyday life, *Emotional Processing* offers all of us new and important insights into the path to emotional well-being.

ISBN 978-0-7459-5259-8

Made in the USA
Middletown, DE
03 July 2021

43592065R00135